MW00463086

THE ANIMAL SIDE

THE ANIMAL SIDE

Jean-Christophe Bailly

Translated by Catherine Porter

Fordham University Press NEW YORK 2011

Copyright © 2011 Fordham University Press

All rights reserved. No part of this publication may be reproduced, stored in a retrieval system, or transmitted in any form or by any means—electronic, mechanical, photocopy, recording, or any other—except for brief quotations in printed reviews, without the prior permission of the publisher.

This work was originally published in French as Jean-Christophe Bailly, *Le versant animal* © Bayard Éditions 2007.

Cet ouvrage a bénéficié du soutien des Programmes d'aide à la publication de CulturesFrance/Ministère francais des affaires étrangères et européennes.

This work, published as part of a program of aid for publication, received support from CulturesFrance and the French Ministry of Foreign Affairs.

Ouvrage publié avec le soutien du Centre national du livre—ministère francais chargé de la culture.

This work has been published with the assistance of the National Center for the Book—French Ministry of Culture.

Library of Congress Cataloging-in-Publication Data

Bailly, Jean Christophe.
   [Versant animal. English]
   The animal side / Jean-Christophe Bailly ; translated by Catherine Porter.—1st ed.
     p. cm.
   "This work was originally published in French as . . . Le versant animal. Bayard Éditions, 2007"—T.p. verso
   Includes bibliographical references.
   ISBN 978-0-8232-3443-1 (cloth : alk. paper)
   ISBN 978-0-8232-3444-8 (pbk. : alk. paper)
   1. Animals (Philosophy) 2. Philosophical anthropology. I. Title.

B105.A55.B3513   2011
179'.3—dc22

                        2011013271

Printed in the United States of America
13 12 11 5 4 3 2 1
First edition

Every life is some form of thought,
but of a dwindling clearness
like the degrees of life itself.

—Plotinus

CONTENTS

Illustrations   viii

The Animal Side   I

Notes   79

Works Cited   85

Fig. 1. Caravaggio, *Rest on the Flight into Egypt*.
Galleria Doria Pamphili, Rome, Italy. Alinari / Art
Resource, NY.   33

Fig. 2. Caravaggio, *Rest on the Flight into Egypt*
(detail). Galleria Doria Pamphili, Rome, Italy.
Alinari / Art Resource, NY.   34

Fig. 3. Piero di Cosimo, *A Satyr Mourning over a
Nymph*, c. 1495. Oil on poplar, 65.4 x 184.2 cm.
National Gallery, London, Great Britain. © National
Gallery, London / Art Resource, NY.   36

Fig. 4. Franz Kafka as a university student, 1913.
Jewish Chronicle Archive, London, Great Britain.
HIP / Art Resource, NY.   40

Fig. 5. Gilles Aillaud, *Zèbre*. Original lithograph.
(*Encyclopedie de tous les animaux y compris les
minéraux*, vol. 1, pl. 43). Franck Bordas publisher.   68

One

I would like to have a video camera set up, one that could position itself on this narrow uphill road (a camera that would know what to do, that would film a car speeding off into the night) and follow me. This is one of those moments when relationships—between consciousness and the countryside, between the speed of a point in motion and the space around it—converge on a single spot: the road becomes an estuary in which one is moving upstream; on each side hedges lit by headlights form white walls. Even if one is not speeding, there is a pure cinematic sensation of irreversible thrust, headlong flight forward, gliding. Driver and passenger alike are offered a sensation of passivity, are hypnotized by the ribbon of road, which may not be without danger. But this time the driver is alone, and not traveling far, it must be said—just a few kilometers to visit a friend in the neighborhood. So the landscape is familiar, as are the borders, the outlines, the paths belonging to the dense woods and meadows through which this road passes. And yet, because it is night, there is some small discrepancy, the soft but deep growl of something unknown. It is as if one were skidding over the surface of a world transformed, a world filled with terror, frightened movements, silent gaps.

But now, from this world, someone emerges—a phantom, a beast, for only a beast can burst forth this way. A deer has come out of the undergrowth; frightened, it runs up the road, trapped between the hedgerows: it too is caught in the estuary. It rushes ahead, just as it is, just as it has to be—fear and beauty, quivering grace, lightness. The driver, going slowly now, follows the creature, watches its croup move up and down, bounding in its dance. A kind of hunt is under way, in which the goal is not—certainly not—to catch up, but simply to follow, and since this race takes longer than one might have imagined, several hundred meters, a strange joy comes, childlike, or perhaps archaic. Finally another path opens up for the animal, and after hesitating ever so slightly the deer plunges in and disappears.

Nothing more. Nothing but the space of this race, nothing but this instant, fleeting and yet so ordinary: many times, and in more distant places, I have seen beasts emerging from the night. But this time I was taken aback, overcome; the sequence had had the clarity, the violence, of an image in a dream. Was this owing to some defining quality in the object itself, and thus to a concatenation of circumstances, or could it be attributed to my own state of mind? I could not say, but it was as if with my eyes, in that instant, for the duration of that instant, I had touched some part of the animal world. Touched, yes, touched with my eyes, despite the impossibility. In no way had I entered that world; on the contrary, it was rather as if its strangeness had declared itself anew, as if I had actually been allowed for an instant to see something from which as a human being I shall be forever excluded, either the nameless, purposeless space in which animals freely make their way, or the other way of being in the world that so many thinkers through the ages have turned into a background against which to highlight the supremacy of humankind—whereas it has always seemed to me that this strangeness ought to be considered on its own terms, as a different posture, a different impetus, and quite simply a different modality of being.

What happened to me that night, what moved me to tears at the time, was both like a thought and like a proof that there is no supremacy, neither of humans nor of beasts, that there are only passages, fleeting sovereignties, occasions, escapes, encounters. The deer was in its night and I in mine, each of us alone. Still, in the interval of the chase, I am quite sure of what I touched: it was that other night, the deer's night coming to me, not given over but granted for an instant, that instant opening onto another world. A vision, nothing but a vision—the "pure origin"[1] of an animal from the underbrush—but clearer than any thought. Perhaps also just a sort of old-fashioned illustration (in fact, I'd like that, all in shades of grey, like the ones in the old editions of *Peter Ibbetson*),[2] but this is the truth, speaking of animals, from which I wanted to begin.

Two

Speaking of animals. I have become aware, stratagems and efforts notwithstanding, that declarations of intense feeling on the subject of animals quite often not only fall flat but give rise to a sort of embarrassment, rather as though one had inadvertently crossed a line and gotten mixed up in something untoward, or even obscene. Nothing is more painful, then, than the choice one has to make: pull back discreetly or forge ahead obstinately and speak out. The truth is that a point of solitude is always reached in one's relations with animals. When this point extends into a line and the line extends into an arch, a shelter takes shape, the very place where that solitude responds freely to its counterpart: a beloved animal. But as soon as we go outside the line and reveal our love (that solitude and that bond), those to whom we have taken the risk of speaking almost always pull back, in a move resembling the one we ourselves might have made upon encountering a similar admission by someone else. There is a very murky zone of affects here, involving in the first place our relationships with so-called companion animals, pets, but a zone that nevertheless extends far beyond the merely private sphere: visits to a zoo or a game reserve, the positions we hold or adopt toward hunting or eating meat ("s'il est loisible de manger chair [if we are entitled to eat flesh]," as Amyot, translating Plutarch, put it so aptly[1]); it is our entire relation to the animal world, or rather worlds, that is traversed by affect and that is troubled and troubling.

Against this affective power, thought, especially Western thought, has seen fit to arm itself, less by erecting self-enclosing walls than by confining animals in vast concept-spaces from which they are not supposed to be able to exit, while human beings are to be defined precisely—if only it were that simple—by the fact that they have managed to get themselves out of these enclosures, leaving behind *bestiality*—condemned as disgraceful—and *animality*, deeply feared, as if these were stages in a journey and bad (though haunting) memories. Whether they have been recognized as fellow creatures, but of lower rank, or viewed as complex machines, but lacking any access to thought, animals have found themselves assigned to specific places and urged to stay there. But whatever purchase—on behavior as well as on knowledge—this hierarchical structuring of existences may have had, what we have seen, without interruption, is that animals have never been able to stay in their places, neither in their own right nor in human thoughts and dreams; the fact is that, on their own and without trying, animals have never ceased to make the border-boundary between humans and beasts an unsettled one.

This vacillation is found at the point of contact, before affect comes into play. The contact is always unsettled, for the encounter relates and even stipulates difference: difference is there, it is there like an abyss, and the abyss cannot be crossed. As Descartes, the theoretician par excellence of animals as machines, acknowledged in a letter, referring to "living brutes": "the human mind cannot penetrate their hearts."[2] *But there are those hearts*, those existences; there is the whirlwind of all those lives and the beating of each and every heart . . . What I would like to talk about is not a transgression in either direction (something that would cross the abyss from humans to animals or from animals to humans) but contact, the close contact, always singular and always consisting of touch, that is the ordinary mode of the bond between them and us—something scarcely formed, always nascent.

Three

"The gods are there": Ulrich von Wilamowitz sought to characterize the particular consistency of the divine in the ancient Greek world with this formula,[1] and we may be tempted to apply it to the presence of animals in nature, at least in lands where they are still abundant enough to give us the impression that they are at home, in their overlapping territories. A presence that is like an immanence: it does not need to show itself in order to exist; on the contrary, it manifests itself all the better to the extent that it hides, retreats—or turns up unexpectedly. But whether that presence is abundant, at once massive and diffuse, as in the game reserves of equatorial Africa, or scattered and rare, as in the French countryside (although night often turns the tables and restores the power of that presence, especially by way of sounds), for us there will always be something remote about it—not only something missing but something that eludes us, holds itself back. The "gods" found there turn away; they do not want us among them, or near them; they do not want to have anything to do with us. Some remain motionless, or pass by without fleeing, impassive, indifferent (only the largest and strongest can afford to do this), but most of them leave, escape, scurry or fly away.

Contact between humans and wild animals is above all this complex system of avoidance and tension in space, an immense entanglement of uneasy, self-concealing networks in which, once in a while, we have the privilege of pulling a thread. It is not just that animals, like nature according to Heraclitus, "love to hide"; it is also that they have to hide, and that since the dawn of time, over and above their own conflicts, they have identified man not only as a predator but also as a strange, unpredictable, lawless being. No matter how peaceful we may want to proclaim ourselves, no matter how eagerly we may seek a slow, gentle approach, in our presence they flee and hide.

And I come back to the flight of the deer that was my starting point or opening feature. The strangeness did not lie in the fact that the deer burst forth or that it fled (deer are fairly numerous in these woods: on another night on that same road, one of them had crossed in a single bound perhaps a meter in front of me); the strangeness lay in the opportunity I was given to follow the animal for a while: that is, at bottom, the chance to accompany it in spite of itself, thus prolonging a contact that as a general rule is much briefer. In a way, I found myself back in the position of pursuer, a dog in a pack, or a hunter, so much so that what comes back to me like an image from a film, like a pure sequence, converges in the realm of the imaginary, like a fragment that might have been dislodged from the whole, from Paolo Uccello's extraordinary *Hunt in the Forest*, a wide canvas on which, in dark green undergrowth gilded by late-afternoon sunlight, the very flight of the prey (doe of some sort) organizes among the vertical tree trunks the vanishing point, the perspective of *fuite*, as if each animal is producing a link in the very optical network from which it is seeking to escape. If this painting is so beautiful, it is not only on account of the legendary material it evokes so spontaneously but also because it shows, right in the field of vision (the forest), by way of the animals that have come from there and are trying to return, the full power of what lies outside the field: the forest, still, but as a world beyond, a *selva oscura* that, even more than the prey, attracts hunters and heightens the pack's sense of smell, because the forest is the animals' rightful place, the place where they have shelter and where they are, properly speaking, at home.

Four

But what would be needed, probably, is a pact, and a pact requires the formality of blood. This is quite clear in Jim Jarmusch's film *Dead Man*, when the hero, "William Blake," a fugitive himself, lies down next to a dead deer on the ground in the forest and paints his cheeks with the deer's blood. Something very simple is achieved here—totemism in its pure state, its native state, but also and especially a rediscovery. "William Blake" was once an office worker, a sort of nervous cousin of Bartleby; now a hunted man, he goes deep into the forest and with surprising speed but nevertheless in stages, as in an authentic initiation, he reconnects with wilderness. We have the image of two bodies stretched out side by side, lying on the material that makes up woods and forests—pine needles, moss, dried or rotting leaves—the dead animal and the living man are there on the ground with water (from eyes and mouth) and blood, and the man confides in the animal, incorporates and entrusts himself to its soul, travels with its soul, an improvised shamanism in which death and life embrace each other in a prodigious act of peacemaking.

Temporarily sheltered from the world of his pursuers, the world of conquering civilizations, the world of winners, where there are factories, offices, whorehouses, and hired killers, the man who has broken with that world and who unwittingly bears the name of a visionary English poet invents a rite, a residue of sacrifice that opens up for him the pathway to reintegration. In a heartbeat, an enfolding lapse of time, an alcove, he finds—what?—*lost intimacy*.

Lost intimacy is the name Georges Bataille gave, in his genealogy of a continuous distancing, to the set of social forms through which humans in earlier times remained bound to violence owing to the harsh reality of the universe, bound to the mystery of their existence, contained as it was in the nets of all the other existences.[1] Arising from the hard-to-reconstitute network of sacred bonds that gave substance to that intimacy, Paleolithic paintings, as revealed above all in Lascaux, were for Bataille the very inscription of this tension; in them he recognized the "birth of art," to be sure, but he understood that birth as the emergence of the very possibility of experience, as the first and most ancient trace of an activity that we can relate to experience. And these paintings, for the most part, as we know well, are representations of animals; while the Chauvet cave paintings, discovered too late for Bataille, antedate those of Lascaux by ten thousand years, they only confirm the Lascaux lesson on this point.

However we may try to interpret those figures of horses, felines, bison, aurochs, the fact remains that they impose the relation of human to animal as the absolutely originary relation: animals are positioned at the threshold of the symbolic; but what is perhaps most extraordinary is that they are there for themselves and as themselves, that is, with the gripping effect of captured life that has stunned all painters by its reality, its artistic and magical effectiveness. Leaving aside the dispute over the sacred to which these wall paintings inevitably lead, we can nevertheless say that they point to an origin or an originary state of designation, and that they can be understood as a first, stupefying *recording* in which, at the heart of nature as a whole, the animal is recognized as the great other, the first companion.

All hunting peoples had to negotiate a pact with the animal world, not only because they depended on it and took from it, but also and no doubt as much because they were fascinated by the exuberance of these beings who lived on earth in a way unlike their own, a way that seemed more *natural* than theirs. (This cleavage must have appeared at the dawn of humanity.) The prehistoric paintings themselves are the form or the modulation of such a pact: through their representation of animals something is taken away from violence. These images *take on* violence as "William Blake" takes on the deer's blood, then they deposit it, perhaps by dint of a ritual action, in a calmed space, that is, in the darkness that has settled back over the grotto.

The lost intimacy is indicated by this threshold where loss begins. The will to have the relation be a bond—a suture, a splice—is what is reinvented, with the gentleness of a transfusion or a tattooing, by the fugitive in *Dead Man*.

Of all that, all the violence of impregnation, no more than a distant murmur reaches us, perhaps. But this is precisely the murmur that was still present when the deer went bounding down the road. Once continuous with or immanent to the acts of life, the contact between man and animal has become discontinuous and haphazard. Whether embodied or terror-stricken, the bond has somehow become diaphanous, even evanescent. Yet every animal, if we will only pay attention to it, if we will only watch it exist and move, is the repository of a memory that surpasses the creature itself as it surpasses us, and where every instance in which its species has brushed against our own is inscribed. The lost intimacy I am evoking comes straight from the abyss that separates us from animals whenever we meet them, and it may be that the conditions orchestrated by the most recent civilizations make the separation sharper than ever before. Yet something is still on the alert, or is still ready to awaken, something that recognizes itself in an animal's gaze or something that we grasp in passing, in a stable in winter, for example, or with bats streaking through the air on a summer evening, or even with fish swimming in a pond in a park.

Five

In fact, they are here, numerous, varied, infinitely varied, on the earth, in water, in the air, among us and apart from us, sharing a world in which they have existed longer than we have and from which, perhaps, they are going to disappear, in some cases soon. (I shall return to this threat: it is obsessive, it is present as soon as one thinks about animals.) But let us say that they are still here and that they are, or have been, our companions, our rivals, our prey, our victims, our slaves, our guinea pigs, our fathers, and also, sometimes, our children. However the relationship may have been established, from the most obscure magic to the coldest economic rationality, it has been constitutive of the human make-up: we deduce ourselves from our unease or our hypocrisy in the face of these other living creatures that are here as we are, and differently, on the earth. The story of humanity could be told in terms of the stages in this relation, with its great ruptures: the emergence of animal husbandry (along with the parallel emergence of agriculture), which puts an end to the exclusiveness of hunting; the industrial transformation of stock breeding, which institutes a relation of nondifferentiation in which animals are negated as never before; and the destruction of ecosystems, which imperils the very existence of wild animals.

This must not be viewed as a great fresco or, worse, as a kind of saga or serial in which human beings, with their arrogance, hold all the strings, but as a gigantic cluster of behaviors and histories, as a mass of possibilities from the most terrible to the sweetest, and where everything oscillates between a paradisiacal virtuality (paradise being first of all the space—that lost space—in which it is not necessary to kill) and an infernal register (the realm of generalized murder).

Here, too, we would want all the legendary subject matter to come into play, all the prodigious instances of contact, the mythical universal presence of animals that circulates and spreads into dreams and art, and which is always extraordinarily suggestive: it is by no means necessary to give in to some wild syncretism in order to conceive of the connections that may exist—that do exist—between, say, "the wolf man" and some transforming mask from British Columbia, or between Anubis, the black dog whose paw rests on the shoulder of the dead and Minerva's owl, which "spreads its wings only with the falling of the dusk,"[1] or between the ass that bore Mary during the flight into Egypt and the she-cat whose sleep the prophet apparently did not want to disturb. The thoughts of human beings from every era are full of animals, no matter what cult they may practice and no matter how hard they try to resist; ever since the dawn of time we have been visited, invaded, traversed by animals or their phantoms. What Gilles Deleuze and Félix Guattari formalized with the term *devenir-animal* ("becoming-animal") is not a cartography of exceptional transferences, not a question of "cases"; it is a generalized exposure of humanity to its original source, a peopling of the mind by that which surrounds it and which it may no longer see, no longer wish to see.

It is not a question of seeing Hegel, for example, with his owl, as a shaman; it is simply a matter of taking into account the full weight that his formula gleans after all from a disquieting strangeness that is strictly animal in origin, and then drawing the consequences, perhaps to veer in a direction in which philosophy, except no doubt for Adorno, Merleau-Ponty, and more recently Derrida,[2] has largely been unwilling to venture: that is, toward a place where animals are taken into account not as objects of study, as allegorical motifs or counterexamples, but quite differently, a place where the suspicion arises that an animal itself is or might be something like a thought.

But here where this possibility can be posited, we have to abandon, despite its richness and exuberance, the extraordinary material offered by the allegorical and mythical power of the animal world; in other words, we have to force ourselves to remain on a threshold that precedes all interpretation. A threshold where, prior to any definition, animals are no longer reducible to a body of knowledge that localizes them or to a legend that traverses them; they are perceived in their pure singularity, as distinct beings that participate in the world of the living and that regard us in the same light.

Six

"And yet, sometimes a silent animal looks up at us and silently looks through us."[1] The eighth of the *Duino Elegies*, a poem fully contiguous with a meditation on the mode of being of animals, returns us with these words to the theme of openness with which it abruptly began: "All eyes, the creatures of the World look out into the open"—Rilke makes this observation at the outset.[2] But with this variation, which has the effect of a light oar stroke in the course of the poem, what is designated is the movement through which, although without coming to us, the animal sometimes turns toward us: it is the experience of a threshold. Rilke says "a silent *animal*": he does not say that dog, that horse, that sheep, he is not recounting an episode but defining a recurring moment, an experience available to everyone at some point.

The world of gazes is the world of *signifiance*,[3] that is, of a possible, open, still indeterminate meaning. For the percussive impact of difference that is produced by discourse, the gaze substitutes a sort of dispersal: the unformulated is its element, its watery origin. The gaze gazes, and the unformulated is, in it, the pathway of thought, or at least of a thinking that is not uttered, not articulated, but that takes place and sees itself, holds itself in this purely strange and strangely limitless place which is the surface of the eye.

Thus it is even among humans, who compensate, however, through discourse for this lack of determinacy and of articulation. But among animals, the absence of language means there is no compensation for the lack, and this is why their gaze is so disarming when it settles on us, which happens, as Rilke's line says, sweetly and soberly. In the face of that which is and can only be for us neither question nor response, we experience the feeling of being in the presence of an unknown force, at once supplicating and calm, that in effect traverses us. This force may not need to be named, but where it is exercised it is as though we were in the presence of a different form of thought, a thought that could only have ahead of it, and overwhelmingly, the *pensive* path.

This pensivity on the part of animals, in which some have been willing to see only stupor, is in any case made manifest in a thousand different ways, according to species, individuals, and circumstances. It seems to me that certain people have seen this, have approached it, and that others, who may have glimpsed it, have turned away at once. There are important and serious divisions here.

My concern is not that we should credit animals with access to thought; it is that we should move beyond human exclusivity, that we should let go of the eternally renewed credo according to which our species is the pinnacle of creation and has a unique future. The pensivity of animals, or at least what I am trying to designate and grasp with this term, is neither a diversion nor a curiosity; what it establishes is that the world in which we live is gazed upon by other beings, that the visible is shared among creatures, and that a politics could be invented on this basis, if it is not too late.[4]

Seven

Animals are spectators in the world. We are spectators in the world alongside them and simultaneously. This community of the sense of sight makes us alike and relates us; it posits between us the possibility of a threshold, the threshold-experience of which Rilke speaks. What is at stake is not beauty but an intensity that can be restored to us: the most magnificent pine forest, the most beautiful mountain, resists us and is inexhaustible; no discourse (as Francis Ponge demonstrated), no image (as Cézanne verified) can come to terms with it fully. But neither the mountain nor the pine forest, no object and no plant, can do what any animal can do: see us, and make us understand that we are seen. No solidarity follows, probably, but there is nevertheless this objective link among living creatures that see one another and are afraid of one another. The act of looking up, the movement Rilke describes, is also a matter of escaping from fear, an attempt at something other than indifference or greed. Something else. Like a new curiosity, new with every repetition.

"To perceive the aura of an object we look at means to invest it with the ability to look at us in return." This is the definition—one of the most famous, one of the most astonishing—that Benjamin gives of the aura.[1] At the heart of the study in which this definition figures, it is prepared by a reflection on returning, sending back: "There is no gaze that does not expect a response from the being to which it is addressed," Benjamin says, making the aura precisely what comes to fulfill that expectation.[2] That is why the "ability to look" stands in for such a response. In this way Benjamin, who is speaking of a "transference," lends to the inanimate world, to certain glimmers of that world, the ability to send back: not in the vague form of an enigmatic force, but in the form of a power normally given only to animate beings, a power that most humans acknowledge only in themselves: not sight or the gaze as such, but the particular accent which is the power to look, that is, the very movement that Rilke's line identifies. Of course, what is at issue is an image; at no time does Benjamin suggest that the thing endowed with an aura pulls away from the inanimate world and comes to life; at no time does he locate himself in the space of a response to Lamartine's gentle question about the "soul" of objects.[3] But this image has value in itself, and it strikes us, as it were, all by itself: what is pinpointed in this way is the radiation of a thing, the entry of things into the regime of signifiance.

But to animals, the power to look is not granted by humans; they have this power on their own. This is to say that, on their own initiative and as living beings, they inaugurate the regime of meaning that is at once, if we maintain the equation between Rilke and Benjamin, a regime of signifiance and a regime of auras. Here is how it works: each gaze—and this is manifest in every portrait—is invested with an overwhelming meaning, a surpassing of all limits within a single point of opening. "The unique appearance of a distance, no matter how close it may be," which is the other great Benjaminian definition of the aura,[4] could also be a definition of the gaze, of what is raised in any gaze that is raised up toward us.

Eight

Recognizing this remoteness near at hand in the gaze of human beings is something we do without difficulty: the human eye will probably always be, for us, the deepest lake, the most troubling surface. But what Rilke identified, in the disturbance produced by the encounter with the gaze of an animal, is, within the context of sharing (we see one another, we gaze mutually upon one another), the division of difference: the animal gaze passes through us and goes beyond us. Why? Because, for Rilke, we look back, whereas "all eyes, the creatures of the World look out into the open."[1] The open (*das Offene*), which Martin Heidegger wants to deny to animals, is, in Rilke, precisely the proper domain of animals, that is, the one denied to us, to us who always gaze in a preoccupied manner, who look "back," in an inverted, convoluted (*umgekehrt*) way. To look back is to be caught in one's own trap, to gaze on the present in an always biased way; it is to dwell in constant preoccupation with a past or a future, lured by interpretation, to inhabit the "world of forms," to which the open is opposed less as something informal than as something free of all concern with formation. It is because animals are beings without *Bildung* that they are in the open. *Bildung*, which is the proper domain of human beings and the means by which they constitute themselves as freedom, is at the same time the domain that has always had to bid goodbye to the other radiant freedom, that of the open. The open is nothing but an eternal presentation to the present, and it is, as such, without past and without future, that is, "free of death."[2] The very possibility of formation is tied to the sense of death, death being what moors men and women to time. For those creatures—animals—that live in an unmoored time, there is no death, no formation, and, moreover, no language—language being, of course, the very tool of formation: mutely the animal looks up, and mutely it sees, beyond us, the open.

As we can tell, all the elements that Heidegger will use as negative proofs, arguments appropriate for supporting the affirmation—for him the essential, central affirmation—according to which animals are "poor in world" (weltlos), come up, on the contrary, in Rilke in support of a sort of "wealth in world" in the animal realm. The open is for Rilke the very space of the infinite wealth of which we ourselves are deprived. The absence of the categories of time, language, and death (and consequently the absence of animals to truth and to the experience of a Dasein) is exactly what frees them, what arrays them in the intentionless realm of the open—whereas for Heidegger the open, whose postulation he too draws from Hölderlin, is accessible only at the price of an unveiling, rooted precisely, in a quasi-organic fashion, in language. It is not a matter here of mere disagreement between the poet and the philosopher—the opposition is fundamental. Heidegger explains himself directly, moreover, in relation to Rilke, and says of the poet, rather drily, that "he neither knows nor expects anything from aletheia."[3]

What Heidegger opposes to the "poverty in world" of animals is not wealth or abundance but a capacity, a tension: a human being is only wealthy in world because he or she is a Weltbildend, a shaper of world, which amounts to saying that for humans there is destiny. It is clear: the category of Bildung is the point of rupture here. The open, which opens for Heidegger only in the glimpse of a destiny and which requires the destinal power of an exposure to truth, begins, on the contrary, for Rilke only in a place where no formative intention has yet been able to penetrate. It is unsurprising that from here on the bird motif should be what marks the strongest separation between the two sides: whereas for Heidegger the lark "does not see the open," the "pure space" that Rilke defines seems to be the very space of flight, a bedazzled crossing that humans can only contemplate.

Nine

"[T]he birds, as if they were the souls escaping from Etruscan dead."[1] Bearing this trace, the Eighth Elegy will continue to be our guide. Indeed, it is from a Roman custom of Etruscan provenance—that of observing the flight of birds in a predetermined portion of the sky called the *templum*—that the verb "contemplate" derives, and thus our notion of contemplation. The augurs avidly sought signs of destiny in the flight of birds crossing the *templum*. As for the birds themselves, they were passing by. It is almost caricatural: on one side, men, subject to anxiety and seeking to recognize, in the free play of the forms of the universe, signs personally addressed to them; on the other side, birds, who could not care less about signs and who fly freely in the open. It would be too easy here to charge the Roman augurs with a flaw embedded in their own era: it would not be hard to find similar preoccupations in any place or time, whether within the framework of superstitious practices or not, beginning with the same impetus to find confirmation of one's importance by looking beyond the self. The destinal climate is also this belief in the *destination* of messages, and the idea that they would all necessarily end up reaching humankind.

But, fortunately, contemplation has always been the occasion of a doubling: behind the narrowly focused dimension of the augurs' scrutinizing gaze, it remains the case that owing to that very gaze the flight of birds, and the sky, have been observed over time. Contemplation takes place only in duration: it is itself a lengthening, it attends to the time that time takes to pass. Fairly quickly, then, in a world obsessed with activity, in any case, contemplation came to have the meaning of a gap, or a withdrawal, and the contemplative figure could be opposed to the figure of a man of action fully engaged in the business of his day. And even though contemplation is an intellectual activity, its reputation has lost its luster in a world increasingly devoted to the torment of activity without end.

Rodin's *Thinker*, turned wholly inward, corresponds to the image of thought demanded by an era that had turned away from all contemplative fervor, an era obsessed with progress and tangible exploits. In the heaviness, the violence, even, with which the Thinker is installed in presence, he left any possibility of pensive, or astonished, wandering far behind; he is the very image of a concentration that needs to look like an allegory of work, the very image, in the end, of a gaze closed to the open, the backward gaze so well gauged by Rilke. (I am well aware that Rilke had the highest regard for Rodin, but the astonishing intuition that permeates the Eighth Elegy is not necessarily spread throughout the rest of his work—in the *Duino Elegies* in general and in the Eighth in particular, there is something like a mid-air somersault.)

But other images, less heroic and less ponderous than that of the dense and touchy man of bronze, might stand as figures of thought, images of contemplative *activity*, images through which humans would reconnect with their own pensivity. The image that comes to my mind, and here we need one contemporary with Rodin's, is that of Seurat's Sundays, at La Grande Jatte or Asnières. Here I think one sees quite different thinkers at work, thinkers who are perhaps only strollers at rest, perhaps bored, ready to follow the flight of a dragonfly, or the passing of a small boat, or a puff of smoke floating off into the distance. And yet it is here first of all, in the isolated, sporadic trills, in sketches of future harmonies that thought is born, or at the very least the pensive thought that may be no more than raw material for thought engaged in thinking but without which, in any event, it seems to me that we could not live.

The extent to which this *minor* thought—the thought that comes when we say we are thinking "about nothing"—comes close, or can come close, to a slope that animals (some more than others, to be honest) appear to follow cannot be measured by using exercises to force the limits of "animal intelligence." What is at stake here is not animal imitation of human mental processes but rather a stable resemblance of which gazes are precisely the echo—somewhat as though underneath the particularities developed by species and individuals there existed a sort of phreatic layer of the perceptible, a kind of remote, undivided, uncertain reservoir on which all creatures might draw but from which most humans have learned to cut themselves off completely, so totally that they no longer even imagine that it could exist and do not recognize it even when it is sending them signs.

Ten

It is in Karl Philipp Moritz's novel *Anton Reiser* (the book that inaugurates the tradition of apprenticeship novels in German and does so in an unforgettable way, by deducing the apprenticeship, the *Bildung*, from a series of existential knots that are formed, that one sees being formed, instead of shaping it in advance in view of the ending, represented by maturity) that we find the most poignant narrative of the possible community—through thought—between man and beast.[1] Anton Reiser (but also Moritz, since much of the book is autobiographical) is close to Büchner's *Lenz*, that is, undoubtedly close to Lenz himself—and the two texts deal with pretty much the same years, the same period—but Reiser is younger, has no past behind him except his childhood. Still a young man, then, he wanders in the countryside around Hanover; he does not know if the world is too small or if it is immense, he feels lost in it, nothing has any stability for him, everything is perturbation, anguish grips him at every turn. The episode that I would like to cite, one that I have already cited or discussed on several occasions, moreover, is extraordinary. It takes place after Reiser has witnessed an instance of capital punishment that shakes him to the core: the treatment inflicted on criminals has wiped out, for him, the border separating humanity from cattle. He recalls "what Solomon had thought: 'For that which befalleth the sons of men befalleth beast; . . . as the one dieth, so dieth the other."[2] But here is the passage, we need the whole thing—it would be wrong to go on summarizing:

> From this time on whenever he saw an animal being slaughtered, he identified with it in his thoughts, and since he had the opportunity

often at the butcher's, for a long time his total thinking was directed toward determining the difference between himself and such an animal. Often he stood for hours observing a calf's head, eyes, mouth, and nose, and just as with strangers, he leaned as close as possible toward it, often in the foolish delusion that it might perhaps be possible to gradually think himself into the being of such an animal. His greatest desire was to know the difference between himself and the beast, and occasionally he became so absorbed in observing it that he truly believed he had sensed for a moment the nature of the creature's existence.[3]

In this passage we are no doubt far removed from the angelic (elegiac!) coloration that was present in Rilke's lines: what in the poem came across as a form of familiarity, so to speak, even if it functioned as a caesura there, is exposed here as destitution: all that remains is a confused effort to understand, to grasp. "Wandering below the unthinkable":[4] it seems to me that Hölderlin's characterization of the situation of mortals is fully realized here, that we are as close as possible to what this characterization expresses, and this time without even the hypothesis or the presence of a remote space, an elsewhere. The unthinkable is presented at every step and with every thought, as it were, at every step of this thought that wanders, but here it is a head (it is noteworthy that Rilke for his part speaks of a face), the head, then, of a calf, that is the mute relay, the springboard. An enigma stripped of all pomp, a mystery devoid of all solemnity, lacking any *frame*. There is not even a stable in view, nothing biblical is evoked, nothing like an announcement or a prophecy; we are not even offered the logic of a gaze being returned from below; there is nothing but this strange, desperate, inconclusive embrace. The nature of the "existence" that Anton Reiser ends up sensing in the creature he is probing is not something that reason would deduce or concede, it is what comes into being when all borders vacillate. Abolishing distance, Reiser eradicates limits, he wanders with the calf in a space without limits, and it is from this limitlessness that he hears a murmur rising, a murmur in which he can recognize or touch what he can henceforth only call existence, a sort of existence, a reservoir of existence.

His experience of what relates or may relate him to this creature does not meet the path of certainty and affirmation. While the stupefied gaze he directs toward the calf is, of course, at the opposite pole from any form of experimental detachment, nothing comes into play here, either, that could be assimilated to a sentimental impulse or to a form of empathy similar to what can be heard, for example, in Saint Francis of Assisi's "my sisters the cows": no tenable community comes to support Anton Reiser, no hymn to the fraternity among creatures comes to reward him. Yet it is owing to this destitution, with this destitution, that the incredible threshold effect of the whole passage in Moritz's book is released: behind the wish to move beyond simple pragmatic proximity and beyond customary practices, what is imposed is an instance of nonjudgment, a *place* from which it would be impossible even to think about values of establishment or hierarchies.

This could also be expressed in another way: while the calf in question may indeed be "poor in world," then at least one can and must plunge down into that poverty and contemplate it—a mystical vantage point here might have me say "contemplate it in all its splendor"—but it seems to me that Moritz is elsewhere, is headed somewhere other than into this type of pathos. The "nature of the creature's existence" is a feeble glimmer, it does not fall straight like a ray, indeed it scarcely illuminates at all; but with what it makes perceptible, or between what it makes perceptible and the open, the possibility *is opened* of a thought about a relation that would no longer owe anything at all to humanist postulations or dreamy effusions.

Eleven

The gaze, even in Anton Reiser's embrace, remains the point of intensity—it is what pulls away beneath him, in front of him, what makes the difference, the abyss of difference: and that difference differs every time, at every encounter, at every moment. Jakob von Uexküll produced drawings intended to show a fly's view of a given place.[1] There are zoos in which a sort of distorting glass mimics the presumed vision of an animal in a cage. These attempts are not very convincing. The eye is in fact not merely an optical apparatus; vision is always already engaged in the history and the microhistory of a life, that is, in the regulation of motor processes, in decisions and operations of selection, in memories, spottings, and, especially, in affects. And if it goes without saying that the buffalo's vision differs from the rattlesnake's, which differs from the owl's, as it goes without saying that within a given class of animals—nocturnal birds of prey, for example—vision changes from species to species (and from individual to individual), the fact remains that all have eyes, that all *see*. The possibility of grasping the full implications of this fact also varies: astonishing contacts are possible, and sometimes with animals that are very small or very unusual, like the axolotl,[2] while with others the circles of fright or aggression are so constricted that it is hardly possible to cross them.

But even if the ability to look is not equally distributed, it exists in a latent state; it is a characteristic of the animal world as such. The community of the reservoir of existence (such as it appears, vacillating, uncertain, in Moritz's narrative) arises first of all with the sense of sight: it is through sight that we recognize that we are not the only ones who see, that we know that others see us, look at us, contemplate us. The major difference that splits living beings into two categories is found along the line of sight, and sight is inseparable from blood and mobility—this is the world of *heterotrophic* beings. Outside of this world lies the vegetable kingdom, that is, the world of *autotrophic* beings, those beings that do not need to move in order to find food.

Twelve

Attached to the ground, functioning like a sort of bridge between the earth that nourishes them and the air that surrounds them, plants develop as nonfinite forms. Whatever its dimensions, a plant has the totality of space around it to grow in; as a free element, air is all the more responsive to the initiatives of plants inasmuch as plants are closely attached to the other element on which they depend, the earth, into which they also penetrate, and similarly as explorers. The reciprocity sometimes found between the structure of roots and the structure of branches may surprise us. But these extraordinary forms, unfolded in series of connected tufts, in superimposed parabolas, forms full of curves and angles, narrowings and expansions, interlacings and protrusions, trembling in the wind through all their countless leaves, however free they may be, remain unfailingly attached to a common trunk, to a nourishing channel that comes from the earth. Starting from the ground, launched into the air, a plant might be said to palpate the world; the form it invents (by adapting its own program of reiterations to the conditions of the specific biome where it is growing[1]) not only has no need to be closed, compact, but it must not be—as though, in compensation for its native immobility, the plant is offered a formal program of propulsions and exertions resulting in an extraordinarily complex and meticulous arrangement in space: festoons, embroideries, topstitchings, and above all the structural prowess that is all the more astonishing in that it reestablishes symmetries after having seemingly disavowed them, producing volumes that contest fullness and surfaces that break free of flatness.

Prowesses, then, of acacias and aspens, ferns and thymes, pines and brambles—ultimately all arborescence would need to be described anew, with the rhizomatic aspect of deployment folded back into it rather than set in opposition: for what shoots up into the air and what plunges down into the earth are fundamentally one and the same. No tree ever looked like a family tree; a forest is a body of perforated veils, and the very site of the highest effusion of branches, the canopy, is surely what most resembles a sponge, that is, an indefinite body or at least one that is undefinable in terms of dimensions alone. The vegetable realm as a whole is a fractal factory, a vertigo of trembling solutions wrestling one with the other in a tangled skein of blind path-formations.

(From this universal definition of the vegetal, only fruits and grains escape. Whereas flowers can look like exuberant variations at the heart of what might be called the fractal sublime [think of what it would take, if it were even possible, to calculate the surface area of a peony!], fruits and grains for their part have no regime of unfolding but volumetric density. From the spindle-shaped form of a grain of wheat to the quasi-spherical perfection of a green pea, from one fruit in the orchard to another, it is like a contest of rotundities and plenitudes: thus seeds and fruits and, consequently, the very poles of what sustains life [which is, here, the pure *bios*], seem to be indexed to a regime of absolute finitude, interspersed, as if evading this regime for a time, in the infinite weaving of structures and balancings that regulate the vegetal world.)

Thirteen

The formal unfolding of heterotrophs is an entirely different matter. Heterotrophs had to develop apart from any link to the ground, and thus they are always, at every degree of evolution, obliged to move. The search for food has led to the deployment of means capable of increasing the mobility inherent in the very condition of animals: paleontology allows us to reconstitute (not without some zones of obscurity) the global film of the morphological and sensorial acquisitions through which animals have acquired the form they have today, the one we see with our own eyes, a form that seems definitive, to us, although this is by no means the case. This form, whatever it may be and to whatever environment it corresponds, is always closed in on itself and relatively compact, unlike the forms of the vegetal realm: beings to which movement is given must have equipment for moving (feet, wings, fins, and so on) as well as the sensory "black box" that necessarily accompanies this equipment, but they also must have a condensed, economical form, relatively free of extensions and prolongations. In animals, at least as we see them, as they appear to us whenever we say the word "animal," form is of the order of volumetric force. The arthropods—which include the immense class of insects and that of crustaceans—are exempt from this rule; in their case, the structuring of life seems to retain some aspects, in the articulated mode, of what we find in the vegetal world.

But for reptiles, batrachians, fish, birds, and mammals, the general rule applies to the whole body, the bodily envelope, the finished, indivisible body. Even if, by virtue of its orifices, starting with the respiratory organs, and through an infinite number of pores, an animal is an eminently permeable surface, in active and constant exchange with the universe that surrounds it, even if the animal itself is only pure reactivity to this universe, it presents itself in the compactness of a nonramifying form; it exists fully as subject. Now it is from this mass, be it large or small, that a gaze reaches us, a gaze ever so remote, sometimes almost lost inside the mass: an animal is a form that looks at us, and this form, which can move us in an entirely different way, and does so, constantly, is the only form with which we share the power to look.

At the end of the jetty that heterotrophy has hurled into the void have come mobile bodies and eyes. At the extreme limit of what the search for food has made possible, the possibility of looking has been opened up, like the reprieve of a sentence.

Fourteen

In Caravaggio's *Rest on the Flight into Egypt,* while Mary is dozing off with the child in the foreground of a landscape that opens onto the distance, Joseph holds a musical score for an angel who is facing him and playing the violin. The distinctive beauty of this angel with a gentle profile has been noted frequently, as has the singularity of this version of an episode that has been depicted so often, but I am astonished that viewers have not been more struck by another beauty and another gentleness that open up in the painting between the face of the old saint and that of the angel: in other words, by the donkey placed in the upper background of the scene, seemingly caught in the underbrush, a creature of which Caravaggio has chosen to show only the head, or, more precisely, the eye. And this eye creates a hole in the painting, just a gaze above the bow with which the angel is playing, an immense black eye in which a faint white reflection flickers. And what matters is not so much the fact that this eye is remarkably crimped, as donkeys' eyes are, so that it could be described as underscored with a thick line of kohl, and that Caravaggio has thus given the animal, in this painting from his youth, a powerfully realistic effect, but rather that he really wanted the donkey's gaze to be visible, and that between the hoary head of the saint and the golden ringlets of the angel, even though the saint is looking at the angel and the angel is reading the score, *someone* is looking at us. In relation to the Virgin's sleep, this gaze serves to keep watch; in relation to the musical dialogue, it serves as a silence, it *is* the silence that has descended upon the scene, the silence in which the whole scene is inscribed. The eye contains the scene's dreamy uncanniness, its melancholic outpourings.

Fig. I. Caravaggio, *Rest on the Flight into Egypt.*

It is never a very good idea to credit painters with intentions they did not have, and it may just as well be the case that Caravaggio simply gave in to a virtuosic idea (of which other signs are present in the painting), but the fact remains that this gaze is there, with its reserved steadiness, its insistence, and the dimension it opens up in the scene, whatever else may be said about it, is nevertheless a dimension of pure pensivity, pure movement, not understood, in the damp opening of the eye that sees, that sees what it cannot grasp, and that, grasping what it does not grasp, gazes without end.

Fig. 2. Caravaggio, *Rest on the Flight into Egypt* (detail).

Fifteen

And now a dog. In another, older painting, in the horizontally extended "mythological subject" by Piero di Cosimo, which is in the National Gallery in London, and which may represent the death of Procris as related by Ovid.[1] A complicated story, a tale of jealousy and error, a hunting accident, the sheer horror of the woman who has been killed, lying in the grass, in the foreground of a landscape backed by blue expanses. If there were only this to see, this dead woman lying on the ground, the painting would already be astonishing, but in fact there are two witnesses to the death—a satyr (or perhaps Pan himself) and a dog. The satyr, kneeling, has put his hand on the dead girl's shoulder and is engaged in silent contemplation, his presence an oddity in relation to the story recounted in the myth, if this story is indeed the painting's subject: ordinarily, a man, Cephalus, the husband, would be the one lamenting the woman whom he has killed by mistake. Here, nothing of the sort; instead, the tender, troubled homage of a faun. Nevertheless, it is the seated dog, occupying the entire right side of the painting, on which I should like to focus.

The story of Cephalus and Procris is full of dogs, beginning with the one that the young woman gave Cephalus, a dog she had gotten from Diana and whose name, Laelaps, meaning "hurricane," is also the name of one of Actaeon's dogs. In the background of the painting, on a sort of shore, three dogs are posing calmly; they appear to be at home in this earthly paradise where we also see many birds. Did the dog in question break away from their group, or does he have a different origin, foreign in any case to any pack, the dog in the foreground, on the meadow in bloom, who is gazing at the dead girl? We do not know, nor do we feel a desire to know. What we see, here again, is a gaze, the insistent presence of a gaze, and through this gaze, in an obviously silent register, the deep, flat brilliance of mourning. This ordinary dog does not have the powers of Anubis; he is not weighing or greeting the soul of the departed, he is simply there, poised to say goodbye, as goodbyes are said most profoundly, without words.

Piero di Cosimo is said to have been an irascible man, who loved silence above all else and who "loved to see everything [in a] wild [state]," himself included.[2] Caravaggio, for his part, is, among painters, and to the point of legend, the very figure of excess, a tempestuous figure who held nothing back. Now it is obviously not by chance that an image by each of these painters has turned up here, producing the gaze of an animal, and not, it must be stressed, in the atmosphere of a rowdy and pathetic animality but in the greatest calm: as if the very gap established by the affect passing from human to animal required a sort of discretion—and even more as if the beasts' silent equanimity called for that discretion and made it the fundamental tone of sadness, and as if that sadness were accessible, too, only at the price of a distress that a perfectly normal and norm-governed human being cannot feel. It suffices to turn to the book Thomas Mann wrote about his dog to experience the abyss that separates such a man from this reservoir of images that traverses realms and species, individuals and their

Fig. 3. Piero di Cosimo, *A Satyr Mourning over a Nymph.*

eyes. Although "A Man and His Dog" brilliantly describes the walks the author took with his dog Bauschan in the immediate vicinity of his home, at no point did the bourgeois master allow his own gaze to descend below the line of sight of a man standing and walking, holding a leash or not; at no point in the narrative, which is nevertheless also full of understanding tenderness, do we sense any vacillation in the certainty that everything is in its place, right up to a house in which—this is the last sentence in the story—"the soup stands waiting on the table."[3]

Sixteen

At one point Thomas Mann describes the way his dog, poking his nose deep into the ground, scratching and panting, hunts down a field mouse in hiding. And he adds: "How does the creature feel when he hears the snorting? Ah, that is its own affair, or God's, who has made [Bauschan] the enemy of field-mice."[1] Clearly there is nothing scandalous here. But when I read these lines I could not help thinking about Kafka's "The Burrow,"[2] or Musil's very brief "Rabbit Catastrophe,"[3] each of which focuses precisely, in very different ways, on what an animal being pursued or caught might "think" or feel, however small the creature might be. No vapid compassion in either case: the moral turn that Mann faces for a moment is not present either in Kafka's tale or in Musil's, but both of these authors (Kafka with many details worked into a meticulous description, Musil almost in passing, in a narrative that is only a vast panorama) wonder what it is like, what it is really like, to be an animal, and the whole force of what they are saying arises from this double anxiety—the anxiety they share, or make an effort to share, with the little animal, but also the anxiety of their own positions, their stances as human beings who see all this and simultaneously see their emotional cursors move over into almost dizzying regions.

So we would also have something like a lesson in literature, or at least like the determination of a fault line running through literature (but through philosophy, anthropology, and the natural sciences as well): on one side there would be the clan of those who dominate, those who will never let animals cross the threshold except in agreed-upon forms that keep them at a distance no matter what; and on the other side, there would be those who are incapable of regulating that distance, those who are troubled by the slightest gap or the slightest glimmer, and for whom the question of the division between humans and animals is not only not settled once and for all but arises at every moment, on every occasion, as soon as an animal comes into view. It would be a little like a mountain with two sides: one without animals, the other where animals are present—the second being the only one, as I see it, that is illuminated by a sun.

Just as there was a *grand veneur* to lead royal hunting parties, this clan of troubled and seduced beings who do not think they can live far from the animal side would need not a master or guide but a sort of standard-bearer, namely, Kafka, the only writer, it seems to me, who has given animals speech (as he did in "The Burrow," but also in "Josephine the Singer" and in many other texts) and succeeded in doing so in a register that was no longer that of the fable. Whereas in fables animals are presented only beneath the words, and play roles that provide a sort of allegorical tutelage, in Kafka's texts animals seem to be resurfacing from some obscure depths, as it were, and appropriating human language for themselves in order to shed light on those depths. With the small rodents in particular, there is almost something like a transference, involving a whole set of infinitesimal notations of sound and touch, a whole repertory of touch manifesting the sensation involved.

But I am also thinking of the well-known photograph in which we see a young and radiant Kafka with his right hand resting on the head of a large dog which must have moved during the pose; the head is somewhat blurry, a shimmering presence in which one nevertheless senses the presence of two eyes. Upon careful observation, it seems that Kafka is holding the dog's right ear in his hand, without really squeezing it. Between this gesture and the young man's smile there is something like a path, a *ductus* of energy: here everything is looking upward and everything is held

Fig. 4. Franz Kafka as a university student, 1913.

back. This portrait conveys a power held in reserve, as if an inexhaustible battery of presence were being endlessly recharged, and I believe—Kafka would surely not mind my saying so—that the dog and the hand on the dog's ear have something to do with this effect.

Seventeen

Isidore Geoffroi Saint-Hilaire, son of the celebrated naturalist Étienne Geoffroi Saint-Hilaire, was a great nineteenth-century theoretician of animal husbandry who defined domestic animals as animals that reproduced "in the hands of man."[1] A figure of speech in his case, but I cannot manage to separate it from its literal meaning: that is, as a reference to the animals that humans have been able to hold, or even simply to touch, whether they are tiny, like birds, chickadees for example, or, on the contrary, very large, like cows and horses. Of all the species, the number of those that exceed us in weight or height is fairly small, even if the contrasts in these cases are spectacular: thus humans are, relatively speaking, already large animals. Quite another matter, of course, are the relations we as large animals may have with those from which we have nothing to fear and with those that we may well fear, or with those that we really have "in our hands" and those that remain unfailingly wild. There is room here for some fairly unusual experiences, those of veterinarians, scientists, animal trainers, perhaps . . .

But even in the most common case the uncanniness is complete. Holding a bird that has strayed into a house, stroking the neck of a donkey at the edge of a meadow, petting a cat on the street or at home, even picking up a grasshopper and feeling it move—these are certainly not exceptional or deviant experiences. All of us, children and adults alike, have had them, repeatedly. But as soon as we stop to consider them, as soon as we set aside their presumed familiarity, the narrative is sure to begin again, new every time—the infinite surprise that there is a being here and that it has this particular form, so small or so large, this form that is also a tension and a warmth, a rhythm and a grasping: some life has been caught and condensed, has ended up finding a place in a corner of space-time; the reservoir of existence that connects us to creatures also passes through this universal condition of breathing and fever. What is held out to us, given to us, is a fluttering, sometimes ever so infinitesimal and quick, with the slightest pulsations, and bones like twigs, but from one end of the chain to the other something unanimous and stupefied passes to bind us.

Eighteen

A German scholar characterized as an "admirable system" the set of means that allow giraffes to compensate for the disadvantages inflicted on their circulatory system by their immense height: with a distance of several meters from the heart up to the brain and down to the tips of the feet, and with extremely high blood pressure, giraffes should logically be prey to frequent fainting spells, not to mention a whole array of circulatory problems. Yet they manage quite well, thanks to a set of regulatory valves that slow down or speed up blood flow according to the position of the body. When a giraffe leans over to drink, for example, in a position that is already rather uncomfortable, it would seem, its blood, instead of rushing toward its neck, slows down from one level to the next. This is nothing more than descriptive zoology, but it is good that the word *admirable* has been put into play—yes, we can use it here legitimately and in the fullness of its meaning: admirable is the extent of invention in the realm, admirable are the solutions that animals have found so that they can go about the world, rub up against the limits of their *Umwelt* and perhaps stretch those limits in the process. This *Umwelt*, which some have been able to take as a strict enclosure of the animal within a sort of behavioral map traced once and for all (this is the lesson that Heidegger retains from Uexküll's descriptions) can also be taken as pure unfolding, and read by us as prodigious.

The open: this just might be the name of the space of such an unfolding and, beyond any specific milieu, the one in which wonders occur—for example, one evening on the Loire and over a period of hours, the perpetual movement of a flock of starlings endlessly forming liquid figures, a triangulation of black dots departing, then suddenly turning back like iron filings attracted by an invisible magnet moving in the sky. Nothing more, perhaps: only flight, the idea of flight, embodied in flight as we see it and as it comes and goes before our eyes—and precisely as if there were in it, in its very dependence and in its pure effect of law, of a law actualized, a condensation of what is not only free but truly liberated and activated in the sky, the signature of pure intoxication with living, in a singular and dreamy beat.

Thus what we capture is a rustling, a pure expenditure that implodes as we watch. Over this image, silent in my memory (the birds were far away, I saw them from a distance, from a terrace in Blois), others are superimposed, in particular that of swallows in Italy, an image onto which the evening soundtrack is grafted of its own accord, the evening streaked by these cries—the celestial well repainted in black over the blue, or even blacker than that, but now by a flock of rooks: and these are like endless sequences of birds, an immense continuous fadeout of cries and rockets, a whole web of impossible auguries.

The open! Flying was, would be, its principle: if at the beginning of life we were offered the choice between flying and thinking, what would we choose? What must be understood well is that there is no lyricism here, becoming-a-bird exists only in thought. Birds do not have this movement of thought, they embody it; they *are* this thought and the wonder depends on this embodiment as well.

The cry that I am invoking or hearing now is the tragic and sonorous cry of the fisher eagle, whose breast is white and who perches all day long in the suspended heights of the great acacias of Africa: incredible, how he knows how to fly and how he holds himself back. The appeal in his cry goes beyond his flight, rather like what happens when our buzzards circle around at great heights in the summertime. Anyone can say that all this has to do only with the quest for food, with impatience, with cravings and the struggle for life, and this claim may even be correct. But who would not also see that at this moment and in all such acts life is struggling on its own behalf, that life *is* that struggle above itself and beyond itself: just as every photographic instant has taken place in an eternity from which it must be detached in order to be, every instant of every flight (of every swim, every run) takes place a little farther away in an open that is still opening and that is more than time.

Nineteen

It is one thing to invoke "biodiversity" as an abstract right, using its abstract name; it is something else again to attend very closely to the multiplicity of exposures and states through which the animal world is revealed and concealed in the vast game of hide-and-seek played out in its native places. Biodiversity, no, that doesn't sound right, that doesn't sound like the infinite declension of the diverse through which animals declare themselves: the animal, animality, all these singulars (and thus biodiversity as well) are, as Derrida has insistently reminded us, simply terms that allow thought to avoid following the real paths of the animal world, paths that are first and always immediately those of a "heterogeneous multiplicity of the living" or those of a tangled game of relations (to life, to the living, to the dead, to the world[1]), a veritable and venerable skein of behaviors and gaps, continuities and contiguities, with leaps and shifts, variations and conjugations. Perhaps it is only here, in proximity to animals, then, that we truly encounter the whole fabulous conjugation of the verb *to be*; perhaps it is only here that the extraordinary repressed, disappropriating force of this infinitive is disengaged from any substantivation, from standing in any sense as a stele. This disengagement liberates not a realm or a grasp, but rather an infinite declension of states, postures, and modes of being: to be a pike, to be a gnu, to be a cat, to be a monkey, and, among monkeys, to be a vervet or a magot, a colobus or a langur, and, among magots, to be this one, in the Atlas Mountains, sucking on a frozen leaf to quench its thirst,[2] one winter day in some valley—in other words, to be *this* being and to be it in *this* way in *this* instant, in the serendipity of this instant.

What is moving out of reach here, what is going away all by itself, is a slope that we cannot follow, that we can see retreating only in thought. It is the slope of every being taken separately in the turmoil of all possible existences: the singularity, for us unthinkable, not only of each magot or vervet but also of each swallow, each rook, and perhaps even each herring, each ant, who knows? Nothing in any case can allow us to say that a single animal, taken at the height of its vivacity, is excluded from being, inasmuch as it is there, whether it is balancing itself in one spot or propelling itself along, in the always recommended improvisation of an end or an aim of its own, all its own, this "all its own" that it in fact shares with those of its species, but no more and no less than human beings or any other living creature.

Thus the children of *phusis*, unfurled in space and attempting to live there, having learned how to live there, the users of the world, the knowers of the world, specialists in a particular corner or adventurers, more or less everywhere, still more or less everywhere on earth: those of nests and those of holes in the ground, those of snow and those of sand, those that wander and those that return to the same spots after years have passed, by following paths totally mysterious to us, the very small, the infinitesimal, and the large, the very large, those that live in families, in little flocks or in great herds, and those solitaries that have no society—so to speak—except at mating time. Those whose existence is fleeting and those whose longevity is great, those that crawl and glide, those that leap and bound, those that fly, and among them those called rowers and those called sailors—an infinity, then, of shapes and curves, an infinity of variations and practices, every practice of the world forming something like a world; I am coming to this.

Twenty

A world, in other words, a speciality and a spatiality: a behavior. Here, the usual observations, such as those of ethology, show sets of little facts that are major feats, prowesses through which the living being appears as a film that would seem to have set itself, just for fun, complex problems of tensions, linkages, fadeout sequences, setups. And, alongside the "admirable system" of the giraffe, from memory and helter-skelter one may cite the agility of monkeys, the speed of leopards, the echolocation of bats, the solidarity of wolves, the web of garden spiders, the ability to smell of salmon, the distances traversed by the great migratory animals, the infrasounds of elephants or the ultrasounds of whales . . . Constructions or systems that are only the most spectacular forms of an immense living building site in which form and territory intersect and propose to every species and every individual the slope of its own signature, so that each one has a world, and this having-a-world is a mode of the world, a taking-place of the world. Here we are exactly at the point linked by Uexküll to the concept of *Umwelt*, which designates the open network of possibilities around every body of behavior, the skein that every animal forms for itself by winding itself into the world according to its means, with its nervous system, its senses, its shape, its tools, its mobility.

Heidegger (in a move directly inspired by reading Uexküll but in which he turned the meaning of *Umwelt* to his own advantage—that is, to the benefit of the thesis according to which animals are "poor in world") presented those skeins as the equivalent of captive systems within which animals are subjected to stupor and repetition. But it is possible, if one untangles them more patiently, to see in them, on the contrary, a marvel of engineering:

systems, indeed, but with numerous threads and multiple connections forming levels, networks of marks and limits, systems that lead, for each individual, to a *composition*. In such a way that one ends up with procedures of intelligibility (heterogeneous, no doubt, in relation to our regimes of meaning) and with accordions of questions and answers, thus with forms of individuation. In the courses on nature that Merleau-Ponty gave at the Collège de France between 1956 and 1960,[1] the interpretation of Uexküll's discoveries is situated at the opposite pole from the Heideggerian reduction. Starting from the notion of *Umwelt*, which he retrieves and analyzes, Merleau-Ponty conceives of each animal as a precise contraction of space-time, as its own singular field: "A field of space-time has been opened: there is the beast there,"[2] he writes, and the whole animal realm is for him like the nonclosed sum of those fields of singularity, or like a grammar—in other words, a nonfinite possibility of phrasings. Every animal phrase is a release and a grasp. To be sure, each animal is caught in the net of its own space-time, but there is always an opening: the systems—as evolution demonstrates—are not closed, and that is why Merleau-Ponty can say that "the form of the animal is not the manifestation of a finality, but rather of an existential value of manifestation, of presentation,"[3] that is, an appearance to be understood entirely as a language.

What is opened up by this is not a debate about "animal intelligence," with all its burdensome procession of quantitative evaluations, it is the possibility that there may be, for meaning, incorporations and pathways other than those captured by the human *Umwelt* alone; it is, in other words, the possibility that humans do not have an exclusive claim to meaning. Clouds of intelligibility float around us and intersect, expand, retract. Uexküll writes of "the unfurling of an *Umwelt* as a melody, a melody that is singing itself."[4] The melody is at once a song proffered and a song heard within the self; every animal has in itself the song of its species, and executes its own variation. This song, different each time, describes a landscape, produces what amounts to a *reading* of the landscape—an itinerary, a traversal, a remembering. There are gregarious animals whose space-time fields are circumscribed; there are others that extend theirs over considerable distances. But in all cases the skein formed with the world, whatever its value of envelopment, will constitute a territory, a world; and the world is nothing other than the interpenetration of all these territories among themselves, nothing but "the envelopment of the *Umwelten* in each other," to borrow another expression from Merleau-Ponty.[5]

Twenty-one

Of this reconnaissance activity that illuminates and unfolds the *Umwelt*, the flight of bats at dusk is perhaps the most striking illustration, but it must not be viewed as an exception or an anomaly. What is at stake in this case is an intensification or condensation of the hypersensitive vivacity characteristic of every animal's field of action. What is really going on? Through this flight that seems to us merely to trace sudden random streaks, the bat, which most often weighs no more than a few dozen grams, in fact puts together a sort of three-dimensional map in which every irregularity (a wall, a reed, a wire, a flying insect), identified by the return of a sound wave the creature sends out, becomes a point or a series of points that the small winged mammal integrates and interprets at full speed. The light, pulsating body, which offers an almost accelerated version of animal mobility, ceaselessly draws and corrects the changing map of its surroundings. In this nocturnal space, more or less homogeneous and empty for us, more or less melted into the dark, the bat discerns currents, caverns, holes, slides, and zigzags, archipelagos that are like so many sensitive valves surrounding its evening meal. So calm in its hours of rest, when it resembles a huge dead leaf hanging, the bat, at this moment, as night is falling, is pure excitability, pure exploratory inebriation.

The bat's *Umwelt* may seem limited (but we must remember the animal's weight, and compare the complexity of its flight and its rhythms to the simplified life of the tick) and yet its flight is also like a dance, in which we can recognize—but in a sort of atonal abruptness—the melody of which Uexküll speaks. No doubt the quest for food plays the primary role here, but in any event that quest is the fundamental tone for every living thing: for every living thing, including human beings, of course, as the Greeks knew, the Greeks who called mortals "bread-eaters," thereby distinguishing them from immortals and marking the fact that humans are chained to hunger and work. But whatever role this quest plays in the bat's activity, the predatory function does not exhaust the meaning of its flight: one sees this meaning in the evening around houses in the country, this headlong zig-zagging flight—in which Rilke, again in the Eighth Elegy, in an extremely well-chosen phrase, "So reisst die Spur der Fledermaus durchs Porzellan des Abends [the lightning passage of a bat makes hair-cracks in the porcelain of dusk]," identified an an-guished feature as well, the consequence, according to him, of the composite character of an animal "obliged to fly" even though it is "womb-born."[1] Rilke also said that the bat's flight is different from the bird's because it entails this difficulty or anomaly, and that it carries something like the trace of fright, a fear that the animal in some sense would have of itself,[2] something that would detach it from pure floating in the open and by that very token would bring it closer to us.

It may be that here Rilke is displacing onto the bat the regime of dark connotations to which the animal seems linked, but how-ever this may be, it only takes us in the direction of a complexity, a difficulty even, inherent in the *Umwelt*. If the living creature inscribes an arabesque around the quest for food and takes its time, this does not imply that there is no room for idylls. Fear: this, at least, is written into the program of all living things. Yet one can no more sum up the meaning of the bat's flight as fear than one can reduce it to a pure and simple functional sweeping of space. Something else is here—joy, too, no doubt—in this strange and perpetually erased sketch that the bat improvises every evening anew.

Twenty-two

Along with the search for food, acts of sexual reproduction constitute the other great vital contraction of the animal world and, in
consequence, the other major terrain on which the vision that
tends to reduce that world to the dimension of instinct alone has
been able to prosper. However, sexuality is no more exhausted
among animals than it is among human beings in the straight
and "instinctual" line of intercourse. Assuming that something
like animal "sexuality" even exists: here more than elsewhere, indeed, we must take the extravagant diversity of forms and modes
of existence into account, and reckon with phenomenal gaps from
species to species, to the extent that we are acquainted with their
behavior, and this is not at all the case for a large number of them.
But insofar as we can tell by observation, the behavior of desiring
animals (of many of them, in any event, and a very diverse lot they
are), far from being reduced to pure fascination or stupor, includes complex rituals, elaborate procedures of approach and se-
duction, and rivalries. From display to offering, from caress to
combat, the amorous drama of animals seems to be woven, like
that of humans, out of play and epic scenarios.

It behooves us here to be just as suspicious of a sort of trium-
phal pansexualism as of an anthropomorphic sentimentality eager
for pleasant anecdotes that have been accumulating since antiq-
uity. While the troating of the stag and the amorous display of the
stickleback may belong to a single regime of manifestation, this
regime (life, the appeal that the living being addresses to itself) is
so vague that it is still better to follow the lead of each behavior
taken separately and see at work in it all that is inscribed between
the simple encoding of the living thing and a dimension that one

is necessarily tempted to relate to the (to a) *psyche*—a dimension that oscillates between ritual (the pure and simple execution of a dance) and improvisation (the invention of that dance).

An irresistible temptation arises at this point, the temptation to evoke in passing the bower birds of New Guinea and northern Australia, for whom this undecidability between code and improvisation reaches a pinnacle. Males attract females by creating veritable little gardens from colored debris that they have gathered and assembled; in one recorded case a male bower bird went so far as to decorate the flower bed made of found objects by holding a vegetable-fiber paintbrush in his beak and dipping it in the juice of certain berries mixed with water.

But just as, for bats, echolocation is only the exuberant form of a generalized activity of getting one's bearings, for bower birds the quasi-artistic display is only the particularly spectacular form of a ritualization found everywhere. Now, these activities and everything that forms and informs the *Umwelt* make every animal mode of being a passionate mode, passionately occupied. And if there is indeed a program, as has been claimed over and over, there is also interpretation: a species does not unfold in lock-step, it branches out and disseminates, takes risks; it has its scouts as well as its homebodies. The will to live, of which the search for food and the search for a sexual partner are the high points, in fact agitates and troubles every animal: instead of supplying animals with a bundle of ready-made answers, the will to live manifests itself in the form of a constant interrogation, through numerous operations (obstacles to surmount, ruses to refine, channels to reopen, and so on). Hence this impression of constant agitation, of nonstop activity that we always experience as soon as we find ourselves in places where the proportion of animal life remains high. At such moments it is as if everywhere around us life were rustling in a process of self-exploration. To walk in a simple forest (but then no forest is simple) is to traverse territories that overlap and pervade all the space around: subsoil, soil, trees from root to foliage, air, water, mud. There is what one sees and what one hears, and all that one intuits, guesses, suspects—some points of manifestation shaped in ephemeral embroidery at the heart of the immensity as stippled suggestions of latent things.

And this is how we have to imagine animal life, the lives of animals: living beings immersed in signifiance, constantly attentive, that have nothing but appearances, perhaps, the always wavering movement of appearances. But what they grasp in this way, the watery texture of signs and signals that troubles and guides them, is all the permeability of the *Umwelt* that unfurls this texture around them. Only their form, like our own, is finite, notwithstanding the changes wrought by aging. What surrounds it, welcomes it, threatens it, is infinite. The open is not limited to the celestial form in which the Rilkean bird takes flight, it is also the borderless expanse of a perpetual happening—it is with the open that the animal in Kafka's "Burrow" grapples, trying to curl up in a loop of completeness that contains only itself and is made for itself alone.

Twenty-three

The sentence I would like to use as an epigraph for a film on animals (I see it vibrating, with the fragile yet intact tremor characteristic of the lettering on film credits, blue against a black background) is one I have ended up putting in this book, just before the first page or the first shot, before the emergence of the deer on the country road in the dark. I repeat it now, further on: "Every life is some form of thought, but of a dwindling clearness like the degrees of life itself."[1]

Because it seems to me now that the open, more than a sky, would be the space in which these thoughts and these lives are possible, the space of what establishes in darkness the possibility for there to be life and for life to be thought. Plotinus says this in his thirtieth treatise, at the heart of a discussion about the existence of forms in the dispersion of the One. He insists here on the silent dimension of contemplation that opens up in this dispersion: inasmuch as it recalls a "former soul animated by a life more powerful than itself," nature (*phusis*) "contains in itself a silent contemplation,"[2] and this contemplation, which is thought, thinks itself through forms, "for nature, to be what it is is to produce [*poïein*],"[3] and it is production that is contemplation (*theoria*). Plotinus is inclined to consider each being ("not merely beings endowed with reason but even the unreasoning animals, the Principle that rules in growing things, and the Earth that produces these,"[4] he specifies in this treatise at the outset) simultaneously as production and as contemplation, as thought that is action and as recollection. The "out there" that he constantly evokes in his work and uses as a device to institute recollection is never forgotten—it is unforgettable only because it is endlessly presented in proximity to the dispersal of thoughts that remember it, which are forms, beings:

fawns and moths, forests, hills, deserts, everywhere we find some-thing like a vast slumber that must be understood also as an awak-ening, an awakening in appearances. Here we reach the most deeply buried layer of pensivity, an almost-extinguished dream bearing the coloration of a wake, a dream that is at bottom like an overturning: the animal, having evaded its condition as object of thought, itself becomes thought, not inasmuch as it thinks or might think (in the end, what does it matter!), but because it is.

"Thoughts": one might henceforth easily imagine this word as the title or subtitle of a bestiary that would deal only with appear-ance, only with animals' power of impregnation and with what can appropriately be called their styles—that is, the way in which each adheres to its being and slips that adhesion into the world like a thought: a dispatch, an idea of form that has taken on form and a memory that haunts it. Thoughts, not as signs whose mean-ing would be reduced to us, for us, in the fashion of birds' flight as the augurs read it, but in an entirely different contemplation, an entirely different dispatch, that of signs gone away, one after another, without a trace, the dispatch of the *ogni pensiero vola* ("every thought flies") on the inscription in the Bomarzo Park,[5] thoughts that fly, swim, run, spring up, go away, hide.

With ears that are pointed, long, short, round, soft, rough, furry, but with hearing in any case always acute, with scales, tufts, manes, teeth, claws, tails, paws, fins, shells, fur, feathers, quills, down, according to an infinity of forms and substances, an infin-ity of productions (and contemplations) that make all fantastic zoologies so laborious, in comparison.

Gone away, embedded in the visible that hides them, children and facets of nature, "which likes to hide itself," living, mortal, truant, thieving, gentle, cruel, fleeting, infinitely fleeting, ac-cording to their paths, their laws, their whims, their joys, their sorrows: animals: *thoughts* through which the verb "to be" is con-jugated, played out, produced.

Twenty-four

The stippled feathers of a peregrine falcon,

the pink and green of the body and wings of an elephant hawk-moth,

the infinite tracking shot of great swarms of birds,

the way ducks and swans have of putting their heads under their wings,

the quasi-lunar face of a skate,

the way dolphins leap around boats,

the extreme, nearly unimaginable softness of fawns,

the lichenlike substance of the tines on stags' antlers,

the way the stripes are distributed on the coat and rump of zebras, Grevy's and Burchell's,

the *opus incertum* of the panther's spots, which could be said to be made of its own pawprints,

the seemingly so playful face of otters and the way the ones that live in the sea (in northern California) have of breaking oysters with the help of stones they keep on floating algae,

the blinking of the eyes of night birds or a snowy owl's round yellow eye opening in the mass of its white plumage spotted with grey and black,

the garden spider spinning its web and concluding its work with a warning thread,

a tree hyrax at dusk sending out its rasping, agonizing cry, while its rock cousin is ruffled by the wind in silence,

the waves of peaceful languor that stagnate around ruminants,

the simple stretching of a cat on a stone warmed by the sun . . .

What we have here is not a poem, but it may be a fragment, and thus a fragment of the *poem of nature*. Now, frankly, who would use such a phrase as a title in our day, when all possibility of candor has vanished, and when animals themselves are caught in the network of signs and images that this distancing weaves? The fact remains that, on the side of names, that is, in the very heart of the lexical underbrush, animals (animals' names) light up crackling flames, as if with animals' names the prodigious diversity of the living were offered up to be heard, as if it were breaking through the crust of linguistic signification to produce a more complete meaning, at once vanished and emerging, a meaning that not only would not startle Plotinus in his silent contemplation but would be a direct emanation from that reverie: what one can perceive in the strange prephrasal elements of the list, in which a language scarcely spoken and almost never written is sustained, a language that would still have in itself something of the Adamic denomination, minus the will to mastery. For Northern European freshwater birds, for example, a list might look something like this:

> *red-throated loon, Arctic loon, little grebe, horned grebe, little egret, night heron, Eurasian spoonbill, shelduck, widgeon, mallard, gadwell, garganey, red-crested pochard, common pochard, eider, common goldeneye, smew, merganser, great bittern . . .*

Or, for bats:

> *greater horseshoe bat, pond bat, Brandt's bat, greater mouse-eared bat, noctule bat, Leisler's bat, northern bat, Savi's pipistrelle, brown long-eared bat, barbastelle . . .*

Or, for antelopes:

> *oryx, sable antelope, Defasso water-buck, common waterbuck, puku, West African gazelle, klipspringer, dikdik, wildebeest, topi, gemsbok, gerenuk,*

addax, impala, Thomson's gazelle, springbok, oribi, blackbuck, gnu, saiga . . .

And so on, ad infinitum, with an oscillation between familiar names and those we are hearing or reading for the first time, and another oscillation between the names for which we can produce an image and those—far more numerous!—for which the image remains blurred or absent. Between scientific language and ordinary language, between the Latin of zoological classifications (in which the impala and the topi, two fairly widespread antelopes, are, respectively *Æpyceros melampus* and *Damaliscus lunatus*) and the names in indigenous languages, through translations, transferences, deposits of knowledge and filiations, there is a whole world of capricious etymologies in which the arbitrariness of the sign comes into play as a simple effect and as a somewhat awkward human repetition of the variegated colors of being.

But it is extraordinary, this patience or this passion that has been required to name everything, even including for example animals' modes of expression through sound, designated in French by verbs that are mostly forgotten. Gilles Aillaud, in his "Préambule,"[1] listed some of these in passing:

"L'aigle glatit, le chameau blatère, l'éléphant barrit, le rhinocéros barète, la hyène hurle, la caille pituite, margotte et carcaille, la chèvre bêle, l'ours gronde et grogne, le canard cancane,le cygne trompette, l'oie cacarde et nasille . . ."

"Eagles screech, camels groan, elephants bellow, rhinoceroses roar, hyenas laugh, quails burble, cluck, and coo, goats bleat, bears growl and grunt, ducks quack, swans trumpet, geese hiss and honk . . ."

And so on . . . But what were these old words, and why are so many of them in such limited use today? We can see clearly the energies that have been captured here; we can tell that the rain of the One, dispersed by language, drop by drop, is an infinite dissemination, and that with fingers pointed and names brandished, tentatively, as with the images we create, we lag behind and beneath all language, beneath its every modulation, its every utterance; the silence of animals and their cries, both effects of their so widely disparaged absence from language, can be valued at least as the repeated, insistent sign of their precedence.

Twenty-five

They all have it, this precedence, an air of seniority, the look of having been there before, and this is what we see when we see them looking at us and when we see them simply being among themselves, in their own domains. Although the pretentious ideology of humankind as the pinnacle of creation implies the destruction of all the respect for this precedence that would normally be due, whether we occupy the position of superiority from the outset, as in the Christian hypothesis, or whether it has come down to us as the ultimate descendants coming to crown the bundle of genealogical lines, as in the scientistic-humanistic description, we recognize the seniority of animals at least implicitly. But surely it would be still more just to pull out of the shadowy hierarchy profiled behind the chronicle of seniority, a chronicle in which one must of course also include the set, both real and fantasized, of the various dinosaurs. And one must consider each animal encountered as the child, the ultimate offspring, in fact, of a genealogical line that is not infinite but extremely long, that traverses like a single thread the immense tangled skein of the living, with its lost strands, ejected from the *bios,* and its active threads, capable of redeploying descendancies and filiations. Apart from any fantasy of biological empathy (the pathos of the living, of "life" celebrated in itself as a value), the manufacture of cousinhood without end, passed along in the difference of every existence.

On this basis, it ought to be possible for domains to be shared, for biological chains of solidarity to be maintained in good working order—for *everything* that exists to have the right to existence, everything that manifests itself in the order of being, with the struggle between prey and predator itself integrated into these processes of regulation. And for a very long time—the entire extent of prehistory—human predators, living on the same level as a world on which they left almost no trace, themselves remained within the limits of these systems, transgressing not at all, or barely, an equilibrium to which they felt themselves bound by a fearful pact.

By instituting the division between the wild and the tame, the emergence of animal husbandry came to weaken and unbalance this pact, but from another viewpoint it can also be read as the birth certificate of a new pact, or rather of a contract—one limited, to be sure, to certain species—that came to institute a continuous and serviceable relation between man and beast in which gentleness vied with brutality: animal husbandry has a whole history extending from the Neolithic (an age inaugurated by this practice) to the industrial dimension and to cloning. This history varies, of course, according to species and to the cultural zones that it traverses, modulates, and uses to build a singular landscape: no doubt the fluid life style of a Siberian tribe following its reindeer herd has little in common with the terrible confined existence of fowl or swine in a factory farm in Brittany. But animal husbandry, inasmuch as it is the background noise of civilization and inasmuch as it has constituted, with herds, with livestock, the very image of wealth, traverses the totality of historical evolution and remains on deposit, still almost warm, in our memory.

Even if we no longer experience it personally ourselves, even if what was still not so long ago a common experience for a city child visiting the country—farm animals as imagery suddenly embodied in noises and odors, in familiar presences—is tending to fade out; the world and the fundamental way of being of what was the countryside (and sometimes still is) remains integrally structured by animal existence, that is, by the massive and stupefied presence of beasts alongside people, and often in close proximity: the Christian myth of the Nativity, with the manger, which is only a sort of stable in ruins, with the child born in the straw, under the gaze of an ox and a donkey, gives the Western world a foundation and an extension for this nearness, for these spaces shared between humans and animals on the basis of which civilization has been able to spread.

Animal husbandry is the set of techniques that have maintained and developed such sharing, that have brought it to the point of shattering and to the new separation that we are witnessing. Harnesses, woolen goods, milk products of all sorts, butchers' meat, leather, eggs, even silk: all these have a history, and this history, much of which has yet to be written, with its actors, its spaces, its extensions, and its ruptures, naturally includes some violence. I have spoken of gentleness, of the specter of a gentleness that would traverse stables and meadows—the gentleness is real, but it is inscribed against a background of violence: being "in human hands" is most often, for beasts, a trial. If for the lost intimacy we may say that, globally, animal husbandry has procured the multiform space of a survival, it is clear that at some point there has been a break in the chain between shepherd and butcher, between milk and blood, and that, in response to the familiarity people often establish with animals, we humans end up offering, by killing them, only disavowal and betrayal.

And yet, when we see ewes, cows, or goats wandering in fields, or even when we go into a barn or a stable, what informs our first impression is not a fantasy of domination or mastery, nor is it an economic phenomenon or a technological stratum: there is always, suspended like a daydream perhaps—but one that would be an integral part of the manna, the sensation of harmony, of a peaceful possibility—a tranquil surge of the world into itself. As long as animals are granted presence in the landscape, there is still a humming to be heard, a possibility of escape (and I mean here precisely a song for working oxen, sung on a leaf taken from a tree and folded in the mouth, the song of a countryside of yester-year heard one day on the radio, and which seemed to come at once from the remotest of ages and from the nearest hedge, dark and close). It is only when animals are taken out, or kept out, of the landscape that the equilibrium is shattered and that we shift to a regime that is no longer even one of brutality, but rather a regime of dark times in which what is taken away from animals corresponds to the very eradication of all relations with them and to the destruction of any possibility of experience.

Twenty-six

What is overwhelming in India (I should really say in certain parts
of India, and only with certain species) is the constant interven-
tion of animals in the decor of daily life, the possibility that at any
moment an animal may block our way. This happens, of course,
first of all with cows, but also with species far removed from utility
(this is the least one can say!), such as monkeys. In the daily reality
of the Indian street, it is sometimes as though the categories of
wild and tame had been abolished and replaced by a sort of una-
nimity of created beings. It is quite something to see cows and
monkeys squabbling over a batch of carrots right in the middle of
Jaipur. But beyond the surprise of the initial contact with this
presence, beyond the habits one quickly falls into during a stay in
India, beyond, too, the existence of other much less gentle treatment (directed at elephants, for example), the upending of our
habits remains, along with the extraordinary visibility of the sharing; the pleasure that comes with this reversal lingers too, and
lasts: anyone who has gone to India no longer looks at cows (or at
animals, at the world) in quite the same way.

My own stay in India (in 1989–90) followed a year spent in
Kenya. But whereas in India, where I was participating in a theat-
rical production,[1] the relation with animals could only be at once
happenstance and everyday, in Kenya animals were directly connected with the purpose of my visit. However intense one disrup-
tion or another may have been, before or after, what came with
this trip to Equatorial Africa functioned as proof—and in a way
the deer that leaped out at the beginning of these pages is itself to
some extent a child of Africa, a sort of antelope.

* * *

Gilles Aillaud, as is well known (though not yet well enough),[2] made animals the essential focus of his painting. For a long time, in solitary pictorial fashion (even if he has sometimes been associated with the so-called narrative figuration movement), he painted only animals, animals as they are in themselves, in zoos, wandering within the restricted artificial spaces that civilization has allotted them. For a long time, too, it was thought that this way of painting, with its close-ups and its insistent focus, attested to the condition of confined animals or denounced this condition in a nonexpressive mode. Even though such a preoccupation was probably never entirely absent from his project, it is nevertheless in a different direction that we must accompany Aillaud, that is, into a sphere in which the silence of painting embraces animal silence, that is, the place where animals, condemned to visibility by the way they are displayed in zoos, expose only their being, their way of passing into being, like dense and compact fragments, like pure pre-Socratic enigmas, or even, as I have tried to say, like thoughts. Later, Aillaud left the universe of cages and enclosures to paint animals at liberty, and landscapes as well; this move, already well outlined, was accelerated and transformed by his trip to Africa, in which I participated.

The four-volume *Encyclopedia of All the Animals, Including the Minerals* was designed as a sort of lithographic summary of the animal realm.[3] Whereas for volume 1, some ten authors, friends of the painter, contributed to the articles that accompanied the plates, for the production of volume 2, Franck Bordas, the lithographer-editor, organized a trip to Africa, to the great game reserves in Kenya, and for obvious reasons it was out of the question to bring a whole armada of writers along. So I was chosen to draft the articles that would accompany the plates that Aillaud was to draw on site and that, with the help of a small, specially built press along with some stones that had to be shipped, not without difficulty, Bordas was to print there as well.

Fig. 5. Gilles Aillaud, *Zèbre*.

All this went according to plan.[4] And what was for Aillaud a great joy—having the moving material before his eyes, finding himself projected into the traceries of the animal labyrinth—turned into an unforgettable voyage for me and for our other companions, too, during which we escaped as far as possible (and much was possible, thanks to Franck Bordas's familiarity with the terrain) from the strict rules, the hustle and promiscuity of safarilike excursions.

It was strange: we were not so much visiting a country and rubbing shoulders with its inhabitants as plunging deep inside and remaining far removed from people, when we could, in order to be as close as possible to the theme, in a movement that was at once very old, that of painting out of doors as this activity had taken shape toward the end of the eighteenth century, and free, in the sense of the freedom that one would find, for example, in the poetry of Francis Ponge. People, of course, were there, scattered, poor, equally magnificent, and I see them again, not only those who, like the children from the house next door coming into the garden to watch me type, were connected to everyday life but also those before whom we passed, mutely, and who seemed to be under a looming threat, one that was confirmed for us later, alas, the country having tilted into a state of wretchedness and division out of all proportion to what we had been able to see. Hence the guards in woolen caps carrying baseball bats who went from one brazier to another in Nairobi's sinister dawn, hence too the wanderers from so many small towns, or the strange silent procession, shapeless and without apparent purpose, all along the immense straight line of the Kinangop Road.

Of course, there are certain places that I recall with astonishing clarity, as if even today it were a matter of finding locations for a film or a novel—baseboards of a particular blue, wire netting around the counter at a bar, a door opening onto a rear courtyard, an abandoned hotel by the roadside, banana-tree leaves shaken against a windowpane by the wind, and so on—but the only *sequence* I had to write, and for which I was learning, as if it were an alphabet, to recognize and name the various forms of monkeys or antelopes, was that of the furtive or drawn-out movements that one saw or sensed in the trees and the grass, along flooded paths.

A bit of adventure? Yes, perhaps, but that is not really what is at issue here. Nor is it imagery, even though imagery lurked at every turn. The regime that has to be engaged here is that of affect, but an affect stripped of all sentimentality, if that is possible, an affect that could rightly be called the emotion of precedence—the emotion that comes in the face of an elephant, a giraffe, a lion, but that much smaller creatures can trigger as well, so long as they are in their own territories, so long as they give the impression of being at home, profoundly inscribed in the writing of their lives and in their material surroundings. What is affecting is this adherence, and the detachment with respect to the earth in which it is manifested (with incredible leaps, sometimes, such improbable gaps): always a form, and the junction of this form with a space, and the mobility of this junction, and the intersections of all these mobilities in the expanse. The expanse that is present, that responds "present," as it can do by leaving the scene, and by taking its leave, as it can do in Africa, with something tense and nonchalant at the same time, a sort of perfect harmony in the wake of a giraffe ambling along and living before our eyes in the other world of the film that it is making in slow motion, with its small head, its immense legs, and the lovable neck that it likes to rub up against the necks of other giraffes.

The giraffe, for example; but also all the others, and each one in a unique film developed differently every day, a film whose scenario—which for the most part escapes us—has in any case no need for us in order to write itself and to register the diversity of its *tempi* and its suspense, its intermissions and its repetitions. A film made of interpolated and simultaneous cuttings, but cut from nothing, arising from no primordial or foundational manna, present, the huge present of the mode of the verb *to be* couched in becoming, the impersonal conjugation of all sorts of assaults and accents: the afternoon perhaps, at the hottest times, in the sort of immense siesta in which the world—I think I have already said this elsewhere, but never mind—is like a sword of Damocles suspended over itself, a world curled up in the peace of its own threatening thickness, filled with virtual designs and courses, trajectories and stopping places, thoughts and traces, an immense expanse of uneasy and watchful respiration where one feels as if one were inside some silent radiation, some flat and diffuse reverberation.

The place from which gazelles still emerge. In the precise fold of their being thrust down on the straw.

And from which, soon, they may no longer emerge.

Twenty-seven

The disadvantage, with reserves, with the very fact that there has to be something like reserves, zones that are reserved, recognized as such and more or less self-enclosed, is obviously the fact itself, this subtraction from the rest of the world to which they owe their existence, thereby denouncing a state of the world that makes of them intrinsically, so to speak, vestiges and scraps. Hunting, poaching, the destruction of natural environments and of forests in particular, the warming of the planet and its consequences for the various ecosystems, from the far north to the equator, and finally the development of mass tourism—all these factors converge to justify the existence of reserves and even of game parks and zoos.

In a wild world truly left to itself, that is, unviolated, as we say, or at least very little penetrated or marked by humans, there would obviously be no need to reserve spheres for animals that could protect their overlapping territories. To evoke such a world is to evoke something that was the unwritten rule, the instantaneous adjustment, for millennia; it is to evoke a form that has given way only during the last few centuries in Europe and during recent decades in the rest of the world. But the movement seems irreversible, so much so that one cannot help sensing, while traversing those reserves, that one is facing the vestiges of a world about to disappear.

The possibility that there will be no more wild animals, or that they will exist only confined or subjugated, is taking shape before our eyes day by day. Reactions to the threat of the avian flu that recently spread throughout the world, for example, all conformed to a model in which wildness itself was accused and singled out:

peaceful domestic fowl threatened by hordes of uncontrollable migrators. This will become the accepted schema—even though intensive breeding and all the modes of confinement (the word speaks for itself), far from sparing animals effectively, have been, on the contrary, the direct origin of the most serious epidemics ever known. Between the thousands and thousands of carcasses burned during the years of mad cow disease and the common graves of birds in the new century, what is taking shape is the psychological preparation of humanity for the necessity of total control, a world in which wild animals will be no more than tolerated and in which they too will be, in a way, "in human hands," in allotted spaces that will be more and more restricted or instrumentalized.

The destiny of animals is perhaps just one aspect, and not necessarily the most striking, of the sort of preapocalyptic climax whose contours are refined day after day. But as soon as the hypothesis of a world deprived of animals (deprived, then of the so-called "poor in world"!) takes shape, as it did in Chernobyl, in what is called by locals the Zone, we see that this disappearance is configured as mourning, as absolute mourning. Not only on the basis of clear-cut biological solidarities (to recall Einstein's famous remark on the foreshortened future of a world in which there would be no more bees), but directly for the way in which is presented, or might be presented, the "thus" of a world without animals, a world in which all animal presence—visual, auditory, olfactory—has disappeared.

In *Voices from Chernobyl*, the book of testimony collected by Svetlana Alexievich (a book that eludes conventional standards and that is for the reader the book of a complete unsealing, a work of naked intensity), the fate of animals is evoked several times. I recall the story of the hunters charged with liquidating the domestic animals that continued to wander around in the Zone, and the way in which these men, whom one imagines a priori to be tough, hardened—some had served in the war in Afghanistan—say that they could not carry out their task, as if they had been confronted with a horrendous injustice, something monstrous from which they had had to turn away, not in order to spare their own lives, exposed as they were to radiation, nor even to spare the beasts, but to save perhaps a principle of evasion, a life, a survival, survival itself, that is, something obvious and untranslatable, something precisely like the vague glimmer in animals' eyes.[1]

It is clearly not a question of comparing the drama's effects on animals to its effects on humans. Everything, here, is connected, and not only connected but dragged down to such a depth of disarray that a bottom is reached, similar to the reservoir of existence that Moritz touched with the calf going off to slaughter, the calf into whose eyes he was gazing. There is a glimmer, or the remnant of a glimmer, and the animal holds onto it, is its mute testimony and its panic-stricken mark, and at the very spot where horror overtakes him, the animal buckles under, but in total innocence. The cameraman Sergei Gurin, whose voice is heard at length in this book, says that his life has been changed by everything he saw in the Zone, starting with the mute lesson and the appeal that he heard, coming from a background of obscure life of which animals are the ultimate and faithful guarantors: "A strange thing happened to me. I became closer to animals. And trees, and birds. They're closer to me than they were, the distance between us has narrowed. I go to the Zone now, all these years, I see a wild boar jumping out of an abandoned human house, and then an elk. That's what I shoot. I want to make a film, to see everything through the eyes of an animal."[2]

What has become of Sergei Gurin? Where are his films? Who will show them to us? And, speaking of films, how strange it is that in *Stalker* (which Tarkovski made several years before the Chernobyl catastrophe) the only nonpoisoned gift made by the Zone should be that of the dog, Egyptian-looking, which appears trotting above the puddles and which the ferryman ends up taking back with him.

A dog, an elk, the Zone . . . Between the stories of Acteon or Procris and the irradiated bushes all history stretches out, all our history. The leaping deer that was a phantom in my night remembers, it is translucid, it is still running: in Paolo Uccello's painting, in Sergei Gurin's film, the elk's life is a thought, obscure, like life itself. It came back and it comes back, it goes around in a loop, discourse is unhinged, this had to happen: our sisters and brothers by blood have kept silence forever. What would the world be without them? The sky without birds, the oceans and rivers without fish, the earth without tigers or wolves, ice floes melted with humans below and nothing but humans fighting over water sources. Is it even possible to want that?

In relation to this tendency, which seems ineluctable, every animal is a beginning, an engagement, a point of animation and intensity, a resistance.

Any politics that takes no account of this (which is to say virtually all politics) is a criminal politics.

Twenty-eight

Between Monterosso and Vernazza, in the Cinque Terre, on the customs agents' path that runs along the coast and that has unfortunately become a nearly clogged hiking trail, in one of the turns where the path goes down a little and makes a curve cutting through a sort of valley, but still very high above the sea, on a rocky ledge forming something like a shallow rectangular grotto, the guardian used to be found. A cat, a simple tiger cat, but stretched out in the noblest, proudest pose: in other words, manifesting what in the feline pose par excellence is connected to an immediate and spontaneous becoming-a-sphinx. Not a feral cat, I think, but rather a stray, and in fact, as the presence of plates and bowls made clear, a cat fed by the nearby villagers, thus a sort of guardian, functionally, at least, or a household divinity: placed on top of a money-box bolted to a table that was itself bolted to the ground, a small sign duly spelled things out, moreover, asking tourists passing by on the path not to give the animals anything to eat (there were actually several cats) and to content themselves, if they so desired, with slipping a coin into the slot. Now from all this emerged—beginning with the remote presence, the kingly remoteness, of the first cat I saw—an atmosphere that was not strange but strangely familiar, although remote, the atmosphere, perhaps, of a very old recollection of the sacred, not cumbersome but discreet, scarcely more extensive than a whiff of Mediterranean undergrowth, scarcely more pronounced than a slight inflection: a thought, here again, and not a thought "for" cats or for a power of which they would be the representatives on earth, but a thought sent by them, working with them, with what was given consistency by one of them in any case, namely, what I can only call a legitimacy: that which between a territory and an existence would form the space of a sovereignty. Any observer of a cat, even inside an apartment, knows right away how to identify the tenor and measure the importance of this space, where it seems as if one is visually registering the abyssal gap separating all creatures, a gap that is nevertheless also the resource of a sacred friendship, as the inhabitants of Vernazza appear to know. A space that must not be disturbed in any way: the instant a tourist full of good intentions approached to pet the cat on guard, the animal got up and disappeared.

NOTES

One

1. A reference to a passage in Hölderlin's "The Rhine": "Ein Rätsel ist Reinentsprungenes [A mystery are those of pure origin]," in Friedrich Hölderlin, *Poems and Fragments*, trans. Michael Hamburger (Cambridge: Cambridge University Press, 1980), 411.

2. George du Maurier, *Peter Ibbetson* (New York: Harper & Brothers, 1992).

Two

1. "S'il est loisible de manger chair," in Plutarch, *Trois traités pour les animaux*, ed. Élisabeth de Fontenay, trans. Clément Amyot (Paris: P.O.L., 1992), 103–21 (in English as "On the Eating of Flesh," in Plutarch, *Moralia*, trans. Harold Cherniss and William C. Helmbold (Cambridge: Harvard University Press, 1968), 12: 535–79.

2. René Descartes, letter to Henry More, "Replies to Objections (5 February 1649)," in René Descartes, *Philosophical Essays and Correspondence*, ed. Roger Ariew (Indianapolis: Hackett, 2000), 296. Élisabeth de Fontenay cites this passage in *Le silence des bêtes: La philosophie à l'épreuve de l'animalité* (Paris: Fayard, 1998), 279. Fontenay's book, an invaluable summary of the philosophical view of animals, has accompanied me in memory throughout these pages.

Three

1. Ulrich von Wilamowitz-Moellendorf, "Die Götter sind da," in *Der Glaube der Hellenen* (Basel: Schwabe, 1959), 1: 17.

Four

1. Bataille speaks of "the vague sphere of lost intimacy" in *Theory of Religion*, trans. Robert Hurley (New York: Zone Books, 1989), 50.

Five

1. Hegel, "Preface," *Hegel's Philosophy of Right,* trans. T. M. Knox (London: Oxford University Press, 1967 [1952]), 13.
2. See esp.: Theodor W. Adorno and Max Horkheimer, *The Dialectic of Enlightenment: Philosophical Fragments,* ed. Gunzelin Schmidt Noerr, trans. Edmund Jephcott (Stanford, Calif.: Stanford University Press, 2002); Maurice Merleau-Ponty, *Nature: Course Notes from the Collège de France,* ed. Dominique Séglard, trans. Robert Vallier (Evanston, Ill.: Northwestern University Press, 2003); Jacques Derrida, *The Animal That Therefore I Am,* ed. Marie-Louise Mallet, trans. David Wills (New York: Fordham University Press, 2008).

Six

1. Rainer Maria Rilke, *Duino Elegies: A Bilingual Edition,* trans. Stephen Cohn (Evanston, Ill.: Northwestern University Press, 1998), 67.
2. Ibid., 65.
3. The term *significance* refers to the semiotic modalities and processes of making and conveying meanings.
4. It seems to me that the project announced by Jacques Derrida in *The Animal That Therefore I Am* is the project of such a politics. Crucially, it is on the basis of an act of gazing—his cat contemplating him naked in the bathroom—that Derrida unfurls the entire reflection through which he displaces and reconsiders the "abyssal limit" (30) between humans and animals.

Seven

1. Walter Benjamin, *Charles Baudelaire: A Lyric Poet in the Era of High Capitalism,* trans. Harry Zohn (London: NLB, 1973), 148.
2. Ibid., 147.
3. In Alphonse de Lamartine, "Milly ou le pays natal": "Objets inanimés, avez-vous donc une ame / Qui s'attache à notre ame et la force d'aimer? [Inanimate objects, do you thus have a soul / That attaches itself to our soul and forces it to love?]," *Harmonies poétiques et religieuses,* Book 3 of Alphonse de Lamartine, *Oeuvres poétiques complètes,* ed. Marius-Francois Guyard (Paris: Gallimard, 1963), 392.
4. Walter Benjamin, *The Work of Art in the Age of Its Technological Reproducibility,* ed. Michael W. Jennings, Brigid Doherty, and Thomas Y. Levin, trans. Edmund Jephcott et al. (Cambridge, Mass.: Harvard University Press, 2008), 285.

Eight

1. Rilke, *Duino Elegies,* 65.
2. Heidegger, *Parmenides,* 157.

3. Ibid., 155. On these points, see Giorgio Agamben, *The Open: Man and Animal*, trans. Kevin Attell (Stanford, Calif.: Stanford University Press, 2004). Agamben identifies all the elements involved and arranges them into an analytics of difference between humans and animals.

Nine

1. Rilke, *Duino Elegies*, p. 67.

Ten

1. The modernity and absence of affectation of Moritz's text made a powerful impression on Gilles Deleuze, as can be seen in the text he published with Félix Guattari, *A Thousand Plateaus: Capitalism and Schizophrenia*, trans., with a Foreword, by Brian Massumi (Minneapolis: University of Minnesota Press, 1987), 240.

2. Karl Philipp Moritz, *Anton Reiser: A Psychological Novel*, trans. John R. Russell (Columbia, S.C.: Camden House, 1997), 144.

3. Ibid.

4. Friedrich Hölderlin, "Anmerkungen zur Antigonae," in *Die Trauerspiele des Sophokles*, trans. Friedrich Hölderlin (Frankfurt am Main: Friedrich Wilmans, 1804), 1: 94.

eleven

1. Jakob von Uexküll, "A Stroll Through the Worlds of Animals and Men: A Picture Book of Invisible Worlds," in Jakob von Uexküll, *Instinctive Behavior: The Development of a Modern Concept*, ed. and trans. Claire H. Schiller (New York: International Universities Press, Inc., 1957), 5–80.

2. The experience of the prolonged gaze related in Julio Cortazar's short story "The Axolotl," while it is the starting point of a strange metamorphosis, is not at all fantastic in itself. Anyone can repeat the experiment with this little animal. In Julio Cortazar, *End of the Game, and Other Stories*, trans. Paul Blackburn (New York: Harper & Row, 1978), 3–9.

Twelve

1. The notion of reiteration is fundamental in the vegetable universe, especially for trees. On this point, see Francis Hallé, *Plaidoyer pour l'arbre* (Arles: Actes Sud, 2005).

Fifteen

1. Ovid, *Metamorphoses*, bk. 7, 795–865; in *Metamorphoses V–VIII*, 100–103.

2. As Vasari puts it in the astonishing *Life* he devotes to Piero di Cosimo (Giorgio Vasari, *The Lives of the Painters, Sculptors, and Architects*, trans. A. B. Hinds [London: J. M. Dent & Sons, 1927], 176–83.

3. Thomas Mann, "A Man and His Dog," in *Death in Venice and Other Stories*, trans. H. T. Lowe-Porter (New York: Vintage Books, 1954), 291.

Sixteen

1. Ibid., 266.

2. Franz Kafka, "The Burrow," trans. Willa and Edwin Muir, in *The Complete Stories*, ed. Nahum N. Glazer (New York: Schocken Books, 1988), 325–59.

3. Robert Musil, "Rabbit Catastrophe," in *Posthumous Papers of a Living Author*, trans. Peter Wortsman (Hygiene, Colo.: Eridanos Press, 1987), 25–27.

Seventeen

1. See Jean-Pierre Digard, *L'homme et les animaux domestiques* (Paris: Fayard, 1990), 30–31.

Nineteen

1. Derrida, *The Animal*, 31.

2. In Cyril Ruoso and Emmanuelle Grundman, *Être singe* (Paris: Éd. de la Martinière, 2002), 31.

Twenty

1. Merleau-Ponty, *Nature: Course Notes from the Collège de France*.

2. Ibid., 155.

3. Ibid., 188.

4. Cited ibid., 173.

5. Ibid., 177.

Twenty-one

1. Rilke, *Duino Elegies*, 69.

2. The English translation reads: "as if in panic fear they flitter through that sky . . . afraid of flight itself" (ibid.).

Twenty-three

1. Plotinus, *The Enneads*, trans. Stephen MacKenna (Burdett, N.Y.: Larson Publications, 1992), Third Ennead, Eighth Tractate, "Nature, Contemplation, and the One," 280.

2. Ibid., 265.

3. Ibid., 263.

4. Ibid., 273.

5. The Bomarzo Park, created in the 1500s near Viterbo (central Italy), is known for the mythological monsters in its sculpture garden. Many of the large stone statues are accompanied by enigmatic inscriptions.

Twenty-four

1. Gilles Aillaud, "Préambule," *Dans le bleu foncé du matin* (Paris: Christian Bourgois, 1987), 48–57. For more on Aillaud, see Section 26

Twenty-six

1. The creation of Racine's *Phèdre*, with Georges Lavaudant and the troop of Rangmandal Bharat Bhavan of Bhopal. See Jean-Christophe Bailly, *Phèdre en Inde: Journal* (Marseille: André Dimanche, 2002).

2. Gilles Aillaud (1928–2005) was a French painter who rejected abstraction and continually sought direct contact with things in themselves. Animals, for him, were not a theme but rather evidence, or witnesses. He was also a playwright and a gifted set decorator, known especially for his work with Klaus Michael Grüber in Berlin.

3. Gilles Aillaud, *Encyclopédie de tous les animaux y compris les minéraux*. This four-volume set of lithographs and texts was initially published privately by Franck Bordas in Paris between 1988 and 2000; the plates were displayed in an exhibit at the Bibliothèque nationale de France in Paris from May 18 to July 18, 2010.

4. Volume 2 of the *Encyclopédie* was finished and produced when we returned to France; fifty copies were printed, as had been done for the other volumes. Later, I published the texts alone in a book titled *L'oiseau Nyiro* (Geneva: La Dogana, 1991). In contrast, for volume 4, published in 2000, I wrote a longer text titled "Le sens incorporé," from which I am taking here not only the spirit but also, with revisions, certain passages.

Twenty-seven

1. Testimony of Viktor Iosifovich Verzhikovskiy, chairman of the Khoyniki Society of Volunteer Hunters and Fishermen, and two hunters who preferred to remain anonymous, in Svetlana Alexievich, *Voices from Chernobyl*, trans. with a preface by Keith Gessen (Normal, Ill.: Dalkey Archive Press, 2005), 96–104.

2. Testimony of cameraman Sergei Gurin, in ibid., 118.

Adorno, Theodor W., and Max Horkheimer. *The Dialectic of Enlightenment: Philosophical Fragments.* Ed. Gunzelin Schmidt Noerr. Trans. Edmund Jephcott. Stanford, Calif.: Stanford University Press, 2002.

Agamben, Giorgio. *The Open: Man and Animal.* Trans. Kevin Attell. Stanford, Calif.: Stanford University Press, 2004.

Aillaud, Gilles. *Dans le bleu foncé du matin.* Paris: Christian Bourgois, 1987.

———. *Encyclopédie de tous les animaux y compris les minéraux.* 4 vols. Paris: Éditions Franck Bordas, 1998–2000.

Aillaud, Gilles, Jean-Christophe Bailly, Hanns Zischler, and Franck Bordas. *D'après nature: Encyclopédie de tous les animaux y compris les minéraux.* Paris: Dimanche, 2010.

Alexievich, Svetlana. *Voices from Chernobyl.* Trans. and pref. Keith Gessen. Normal, Ill.: Dalkey Archive Press, 2005.

Bailly, Jean-Christophe. *L'oiseau Nyiro.* Geneva: La Dogana, 1991.

———. *Phèdre en Inde: Journal.* Marseille: André Dimanche, 2002.

Bailly, Jean-Christophe, ed. *La légende dispersée.* Paris: Christian Bourgois, 2001.

Bataille, Georges. *Theory of Religion.* Trans. Robert Hurley. New York: Zone Books, 1989.

Benjamin, Walter. *Charles Baudelaire: A Lyric Poet in the Era of High Capitalism.* Trans. Harry Zohn. London: New Left Books, 1973.

———. *The Work of Art in the Age of Its Technological Reproducibility.* Ed. Michael W. Jennings, Brigid Doherty, and Thomas Y. Levin. Trans. Edmund Jephcott et al. Cambridge, Mass.: Harvard University Press, 2008.

Cortazar, Julio. "The Axolotl." In *End of the Game, and Other Stories,* trans. Paul Blackburn, 3–9. New York: Harper & Row, 1978 (1967).

Deleuze, Gilles, and Félix Guattari. *A Thousand Plateaus: Capitalism and Schizophrenia.* Trans. with a Foreword by Brian Massumi. Minneapolis: University of Minnesota Press, 1987.

Derrida, Jacques. *The Animal That Therefore I Am*. Ed. Marie-Louise Mallet. Trans. David Wills. New York: Fordham University Press, 2008.

Descartes, René. Letter to Henry More, "Replies to Objections (5 February 1649}." In *Philosophical Essays and Correspondence*, ed. Roger Ariew, 292–97. Indianapolis: Hackett, 2000.

Digard, Jean-Pierre. *L'homme et les animaux domestiques*. Paris: Fayard, 1990.

Fontenay, Élisabeth de. *Le silence des bêtes: La philosophie à l'épreuve de l'animalité*. Paris: Fayard, 1998.

Hallé, Francis. *Plaidoyer pour l'arbre*. Arles: Actes Sud, 2005.

Hegel, Georg Wilhelm Friedrich. "Preface." *Hegel's Philosophy of Right*, trans. T. M. Knox, 1–13. London: Oxford University Press, 1967 (1952).

Heidegger, Martin. *Parmenides*. Trans. André Schuwer and Richard Rojcewicz. Bloomington: Indiana University Press, 1992.

Hölderlin, Friedrich. "Anmerkungen zur Antigonae." In *Die Trauerspiele des Sophokles*, trans. Friedrich Hölderlin, 1: 89–103. Frankfurt am Main: Friedrich Wilmans, 1804.

———. "The Rhine." In *Poems and Fragments*, trans. Michael Hamburger, 409–21. Cambridge: Cambridge University Press, 1980 (1966).

Kafka, Franz. "The Burrow." Trans. Willa and Edwin Muir. In *The Complete Stories*, ed. Nahum N. Glazer, 325–59. New York: Schocken Books, 1988.

Lamartine, Alphonse de. "Milly ou le pays natal." In *Harmonies poétiques et religieuses*, bk. 3 of *Oeuvres poétiques complètes*. Ed. Marius-Francois Guyard. Paris: Gallimard, 1963.

Mann, Thomas. "A Man and His Dog." In *Death in Venice and Other Stories*, trans. H. T. Lowe-Porter, 217–91. New York: Vintage Books, 1954.

Maurier, George du. *Peter Ibbetson*. New York: Harper & Brothers, 1992.

Merleau-Ponty, Maurice. *Nature: Course Notes from the Collège de France*. Ed. Dominique Séglard. Trans. Robert Vallier. Evanston, Ill.: Northwestern University Press, 2003.

Moritz, Karl Philipp. *Anton Reiser: A Psychological Novel*. Trans. John R. Russell. Columbia, S.C.: Camden House, 1997.

Musil, Robert. "Rabbit Catastrophe." In *Posthumous Papers of a Living Author*, trans. Peter Wortsman, 25–27. Hygiene, Colo.: Eridanos Press, 1987.

Ovid. *Metamorphoses V–VIII*. Ed. and trans. D. E. Hill. Warminster: Aris & Phillips, 1992.

Plotinus. *The Enneads*. Trans. Stephen MacKenna. Burdett, N.Y.: Larson Publications, 1992.